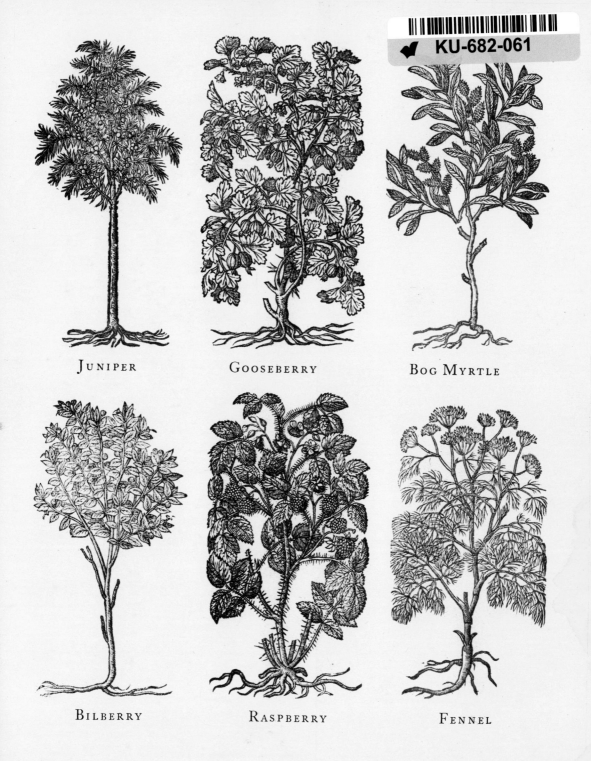

JUNIPER

GOOSEBERRY

BOG MYRTLE

BILBERRY

RASPBERRY

FENNEL

KU-682-061

❦ A Country Cup ❧

JUNIPER   GOOSEBERRY   BOG MYRTLE

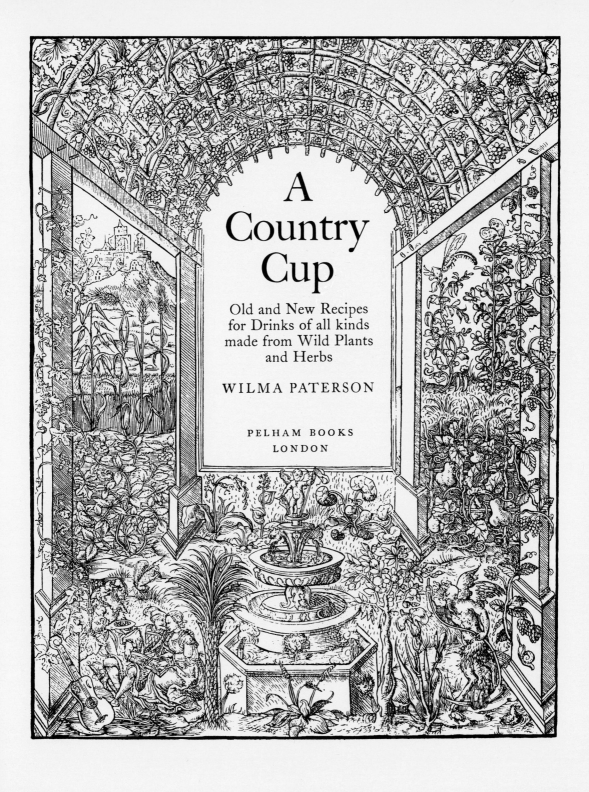

A Country Cup

Old and New Recipes
for Drinks of all kinds
made from Wild Plants
and Herbs

WILMA PATERSON

PELHAM BOOKS
LONDON

FOR JOHN

First published in Great Britain by
PELHAM BOOKS LTD
44 Bedford Square
London WC1B 3DU
1980

Copyright © Wilma Paterson 1980

All Rights Reserved. No part of this publication
may be reproduced, stored in a retrieval system,
or transmitted, in any form or by any means,
electronic, or mechanical, photocopying, recording
or otherwise without the prior permission of
the Copyright owner

Illustrations from *Flora Londinensis* by William
Curtis and *Sylva, or a Discourse of Forest-Trees*
by John Evelyn reproduced by kind permission
of the Librarian and Keeper of the Hunterian
Books and Manuscripts, Glasgow University;
illustrations from *The Herbal or General Historie
of Plants* by John Gerard reproduced by kind
permission of the National Library of Scotland

ISBN 0 7207 1234 3

Typeset in Monotype Caslon by
Ebenezer Baylis & Son Ltd
The Trinity Press, Worcester, and London;
printed and bound by
New Interlitho Spa, Milan

❧ Contents ☙

THE PLANTS AND RECIPES

❧ Preface ❧

Living by the sea in wild and remote country, I no longer take the land for granted. In a place where anything that grows has a struggle to survive, the trees and plants seem doubly precious, for it is their tenacity which holds the land together through the weeks of rain and the inundations of high tides and on-shore winds.

The smells of the sea have a strange attraction — a sort of temptation to anarchy — but the smells of the land are familiar, personal and reassuring. So, over the years, I have collected recipes which preserve the smell and flavour of the wild plants around me: some to keep cool by in summer, others to warm up with in winter; and all of them because the nearest place to buy things to drink is fifteen miles away along a tortuous single-track road. But I still use these recipes when we are in the city because they produce far better beers and teas than you can ever buy and at a fraction of the cost. In any case, many of the drinks in this book, though easily made, delicious to take and attractive to look at, cannot be bought at all. Even if they were all available and cheap I would still continue to make them myself just for the pleasure of finding the plants and learning more about them. Every walk, be it a day's outing from the city or a long expedition among the Skye hills, takes on a new interest as varied as the plants and conditions in which they survive. Of course most of them grow better in the south, and I have chosen for this book plants which are within virtually everyone's reach. Indeed, for some of them you would hardly have to travel at all, were it not for the pollution in the cities and by the main roads.

Here in Skye pollution is hardly a problem; on the other hand, nature is not what you would call abundant. Every year the elder trees produce a sparse crop of berries, and every year, just before they struggle to maturity, they are torn off the branches by the first of the autumn gales. So, for us, elderberry wine is not to be taken for granted. But there is not a place in these islands which does not favour one plant or another, or in which, for example, the dandelion and the nettle have not found a hold; so, wherever you are, or wherever you go, I hope you will find this book a useful guide to the pleasures of drinking from a country cup.

WILMA PATERSON
1979

BRAMBLE

Introduction

All the plants in this book grow wild in the British Isles: most are common everywhere, a few are local and many are worth growing in the garden. Cultivation will produce straighter, fleshier roots for plants such as chicory and dandelion, but otherwise it is hard to improve on the plant's own choice of soil and situation.

GATHERING PLANTS

Pick plants for use in the following recipes on a dry and preferably sunny day, not too early and not too late or they may be damp with dew and liable to spoil. Roots, on the other hand, can be more easily pulled up after rain. They should be collected at the end of autumn.

Take care not to crush or squeeze your plants while gathering them, avoid blemished leaves or flowers and use them as soon as possible, unless you intend to dry them for the future. Remember that if you strip growing plants of too many of their leaves or flowers you may kill them, or prevent their seeds or fruit from coming to maturity. It is also in your own interest, as well as that of future generations, not to collect too many roots or plants from one particular area. None of the plants in this book is protected by the Conservation of Wild Creatures and Wild Plants Act (1975), but you may only uproot wild plants if you are the owner or occupier of the land on which they are growing, or have permission from the owner to do so.

DRYING PLANTS

Spread them out in a single layer on sheets of paper in a well-ventilated place. Turn them frequently and, when they are absolutely dry, strip the leaves or flowers from the stems and store them in glass jars away from the light. Never wash your plants before drying; only make sure you gather them in unpolluted places, free from insecticides and car exhaust fumes. Nuts and seeds should be de-husked and laid out on a tray to dry before storage in glass jars.

HINTS ON WINE AND BEER MAKING

All the recipes in this book give an outline of the processes, though some of the Victorian ones may require a little commonsense adaptation – usually a division of the ingredients for recipes requiring large amounts of brandy, etc; or the use of an appropriate wine yeast to ensure proper fermentation. Scrupulous cleanliness is essential.

In recipes in which fresh plants are to be measured by volume rather than weight (e.g. in pints) ensure that the measure is filled to the top, with the plants pressed only lightly down.

Wines

Your most important piece of equipment is a non-metallic fermenting vessel – plastic, glass, glazed earthenware or a wooden cask – to which you can fit an airlock. In the case of plastic be sure it is white in colour and of good quality, and never keep a wine fermenting in the one plastic container for more than six months without changing it. Wine vessels should be sterilised by rinsing thoroughly with a solution of two Camden tablets (sodium metabisulphate) and half a teaspoon of citric acid per pint of water. You can use it for several rinsings.

A constant temperature of about 65°F/18°C day *and* night, plus the use of a wine yeast and nutrient, should guarantee proper fermentation. Baker's yeast is usable for wines, but it tends to give inferior results. Don't add your yeast and nutrient until you are sure the temperature is blood heat or less. As a general rule, as soon as you see a firm, clear deposit you should rack (siphon off) your wine into a fresh container. Be patient. Some wines take over a year to clear completely naturally; some never clear fully at all but are good to drink just the same; and some don't taste good until after a year or two of maturing. Don't expect them to taste like grape wines; they have their own characters and attractions. A less successful wine may be rescued by blending or by mulling. Decant your wine beforehand if you think there is any risk of a deposit becoming unsettled.

Beers and Ales

A fermenting vessel is required, as for wine. Use brewer's yeast, dried or fresh, with the same provisos about temperature as for wine yeasts, but of course you don't use an airlock and you bottle after about six or seven days. Make sure the tops are really airtight. Be careful with old internal-screw-top bottles. The new tops are moulded slightly shorter and don't screw down so well. We keep the old tops and put on new washers.

Don't forget to add sugar to the bottles, a level teaspoon for 1-pint bottles and a rounded one for 1-quart bottles, making sure the sugar gets dissolved in the beer. Always have a large jug ready for decanting as a good home brew can sometimes be very lively and take a while to settle: it can also be very strong, so be careful if you're driving and don't over-ply innocent guests. If, as sometimes happens, your beer has become too strong through keeping, you can try mulling it as this drives off a lot of the alcohol.

❧ The Plants and Recipes ❧

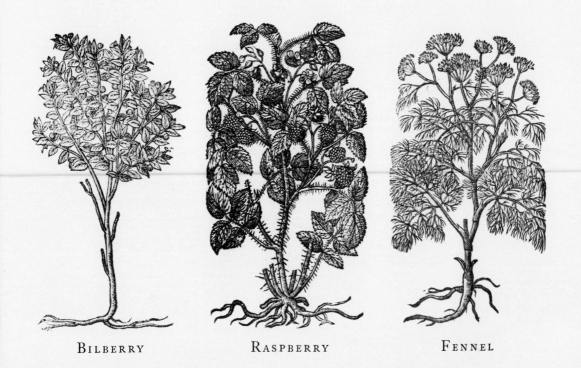

BILBERRY   RASPBERRY   FENNEL

❧ Agrimony ☙

Agrimonia eupatoria (Rosaceae)

Common on waste ground, hedge banks, by the sides of roads and fields throughout England and Wales, but more local in Scotland. I found it by the shore on Skye, growing among brambles.

It is less well known than some of the other tea plants, but both flowers and leaves make a fragrant tea which old people of the Appalachians described as tasting like 'apples with cinnamon' or 'spice tea'. The whole plant is slightly aromatic and the spikes of yellow flowers give out a refreshing, spicy odour which they retain well when dried, as do the leaves. Gerard says: 'A decoction of the leaves of Egrimony is good for them that have naughty livers.' It is still taken in France (where it is known as *herbe de Saint-Guillaume*) though I doubt if their livers are any naughtier than ours.

Agrimony was sometimes infused with other plants in spring-time and used as a tonic and purifier of the blood, or boiled in whey and taken as a cooling 'diet-drink'. An old English medical manuscript mentions an interesting use for it:

Ffor To Slepe Wel
Quo so may not slepe wel
Take egrimonye a fayre del
And lay it under his heed on nyth
And it schall hym do slepe aryth,
For of his slepe schall he nozt waken
Tyll it be fro under his heed takyn.

AGRIMONY TEA
(Victorian recipe)

Pour 1 pint of boiling water on 1 oz of the fresh tops of agrimony (gathered before the flowers are formed) and 1 oz of liquorice root, sliced; macerate for one hour in a close vessel and a warm situation; then strain for use. Good for skin and liver disorders, taken two or three times a day.

AGRIMONY WINE

Large bunch of agrimony
1 gal water
3 oranges
2 lemons
¼ oz bruised root ginger
3 lb sugar
wine yeast and nutrient

Boil the agrimony in the water with the bruised ginger for ten minutes. Strain on to the sugar and the sliced oranges and lemons (first removing the white pith as this gives a bitter taste). When cool, add the yeast and nutrient, cover, and leave for two days, stirring occasionally. Strain into a fermentation jar, fit an airlock, and leave to ferment in a warm place. Rack once or twice if necessary before finally bottling the wine.

Agrimonia Eupatoria

AGRIMONY

❧ Angelica ❧

Angelica archangelica; Angelica sylvestris (Umbelliferae)

A. archangelica (or *A. officinalis*) is seldom found native in this country, but more often further north, as in Lapland where it is eaten raw in salads. However, wild angelica (*A. sylvestris*) is fairly common in damp meadows, woods, and shady places throughout Britain. It is smaller and less aromatic, but gives a good yellow dye. *A. archangelica* is well worth growing in the garden – it is a magnificent ornamental plant, growing to about six feet. In the seventeenth century it was so common that Culpeper thought it unnecessary to describe it. Of its name he says, '. . . some call this an herb of the Holy Ghost; others more moderate called it Angelica, because of its angelical virtues, and that name it retains still, and all nations follow it so near as their dialect will permit.'

The seed must be sown when very fresh – that is, just as soon as it is ripe at the end of August or beginning of September. If you wish to keep the plant as a perennial you should follow Gerard's advice as it will normally die in its third year when it has produced seed: 'They floure in July and August, whose roots for the most part do perish after the seed is ripe: yet have I with often cutting the plant kept it from seeding, by which meanes the root and plant have continued sundry years together.'

Angelica was valued as a remedy against the plague, poisons and even as a protection against witchcraft, if you carried the dried root about your person. Now it is mainly used in confectionery (it is well worth candying your own stems) and as a flavouring in drinks such as chartreuse, vermouths and various Italian liqueurs.

ANGELICA RATAFIA
(Victorian recipe)

Strip the angelica stalks of their leaves, and cut them into small pieces, which put into the best brandy and water in the proportion of 8 pints of brandy and 4 pints of water to 1 lb of angelica, and 4 lb of sugar; add $\frac{1}{4}$ oz of cloves and cinnamon mixed in equal proportions; let it stand for six weeks, then filter and bottle it.

ANGELICA TEA

Cut the young leaves in early summer and dry for use all the year round. Make an infusion, as you would with China tea, and drink hot or cold, sweetened with honey. You can, of course, use the leaves fresh and, as for all teas, the sweetening is a matter of personal taste.

ANGELICA LIQUEUR

Chop up 1 oz of freshly gathered angelica stems and steep in 2 pints of good brandy for five days. Add 1 oz of skinned and powdered bitter almonds. Strain through fine muslin and add 1 pint of liquid sugar.

ANGELICA PUNCH
(French recipe)

Pour 1 pint of boiling water on to 1 oz of chopped angelica root. When cool add $\frac{1}{2}$ pint of white rum and serve chilled with slices of lemon.

❧ Balm ☙

Melissa officinalis (Labiatae)

An introduced perennial from southern Europe, balm is naturalised in the south of England in Cornwall and Devon and also in South Wales. Gerard writes: 'Bawme is much sowen and set in gardens, and oftentimes it groweth of itself in woods and mountaines, and other wilde places: it is profitably planted in gardens as Pliny writes, lib:21, cap:12, about places where Bees are kept, because they are delighted with this herb above others, whereupon it hath bene called *Apiastrum*: for, saith he, when they are strayed away, they do find their way home againe by it.' Beekeepers still use balm rubbed on the hives to attract stray swarms.

Like borage, balm was taken to relieve melancholy, and Thomas Cogan, an Oxford don of the sixteenth century, recommends the distilled water of balm, borage and bugloss to his students. Evelyn, in the next century, also writes in praise of balm: 'Balm is sovereign for the brain, strengthening the memory and powerfully chasing away melancholy.' It is easily grown anywhere, in a flower pot, window box or garden; it dies down in winter but is a perennial and a useful and fragrant plant, giving out a delicious lemon scent when the leaves are touched. Drinks made with the leaves are very refreshing and said to be good for fevers in colds and 'flu, and against 'the bitings of venemous beasts' (Gerard) –

But soon as e'er the beauteous idiot spoke,
Forth from her coral lips such folly broke,
Like balm the trickling nonsense heal'd my
*   wound,*
And what her eyes enthral'd, her tongue
*   unbound.*

(Congreve: *Lesbia*)

BALM TEA

Pour 1 pint of boiling water on 1 oz of the herb. Infuse for ten minutes, strain, and add honey and lemon to taste. (The fresh leaves make a better tea than the dried.)

CLARET CUP
(Recipe used by C. E. Francatelli, Queen Victoria's chef)

1 bottle of claret, 1 pint bottle of German Seltzer-water [or other mineral water], a small bunch of Balm, ditto of burrage, one orange cut in slices, half a cucumber sliced thick, a liqueur-glass of Cognac, and 1 oz of bruised sugar-candy. Place these ingredients in a covered jug well immersed in rough ice, stir all together with a silver spoon, and when the cup has been iced for about an hour, strain or decanter it off from the herbs, etc.

BALM WINE

½ gal balm leaves
1 lb raisins
2¾ lb sugar
1 gal water
1 lemon
1 orange
1 tablespoon tea
wine yeast and nutrient

Bruise the leaves and place in a crock with the raisins, sugar, tea, juice and thinly-pared rinds of orange and lemon (leave out any pith). Add

[15]

the boiling water and, when cool, the yeast and nutrient. Cover and leave in a warm place for a week, then siphon off into a fermentation jar, fit an airlock and leave until fermentation has ceased. When clear, siphon off into clean bottles.

❧ Barley ❧

Hordeum murinum (Gramineae)

Wild barley is very common all over the British Isles, but the prepared pot or polished pearl barley is cheaply and easily obtained, being still a basic ingredient for broth in many places. Barley meal – barley ground into flour – was commonly used to make scones or bannocks. Pot barley, or Scotch barley, has had the outer skin removed; pearl is the small, round kernel remaining after the skin and a considerable quantity of the grain have been ground off. In Holland pot barley, boiled in buttermilk and sweetened with treacle, used to be a common dish for children and servants, and in England the cereal was boiled with raisins, currants or prunes to make a barley broth or gruel. A richer version of this with rosewater, white wine, butter and sugar was said to have been a favourite of Oliver Cromwell.

Culpeper gives many uses for barley, both internal and external, and no doubt Robinson & Co. would agree with him that ' . . . all the preparations thereof, as barley water and other things made thereof, do give nourishment to persons troubled with fevers, agues and heats in the stomach'. Malted barley is the basis of our beers and whiskies, the drying of the malt over a fragrant peat fire giving Highland whisky its distinctive smoky flavour.

BARLEY COFFEE

Roast pot barley on a baking sheet in a hot oven until very dark brown, but taking care that it does not burn. Grind in a coffee grinder and use as ground coffee, either by itself or mixed with real coffee.

LEMON BARLEY WATER
(Med Dods' recipe)

Wash common or pearl barley, and take in the proportion of an ounce to a quart of water. Give it a boil for a few minutes in a very little water, and strain off this, and take fresh water, which will make the barley water lighter and of a better colour. Boil it down one half. Lemon peel and sugar may be added, or a compound draught made, by adding to every pint of the decoction an ounce of stoned raisins, a quarter ounce of sliced liquorice root and 3 or 4 figs. With lemon juice it is less cloying and more grateful to the sick. Currant jelly answers very well in barley water.

BARLEY WINE

1 lb pot barley
1 lb potatoes
1 lb raisins

[16]

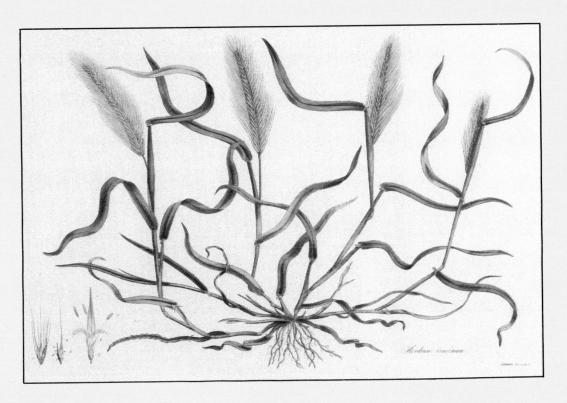

Hordeum murinum

BARLEY

3 lb white sugar
1 gal water
2 lemons
wine yeast and nutrient
1 Camden tablet

Soak the grain overnight. Scrub and chop the potatoes. Put the barley, potatoes, raisins and sugar into a jar and pour on the hot water. Add the juice of the lemons. Allow to cool until tepid, then add the crushed Camden tablet, yeast and nutrient. Cover the jar and leave it to stand for ten days, stirring well daily. Strain, put into a fermentation jar and fit an airlock. Siphon off into bottles when clear and fermen-tation has ceased. Ready after six months.

Barley Posset
(Victorian recipe)

Boil 1 lb. of barley in 3 quarts of milk; when boiled enough, put in 3 quarts of cream, some cinnamon and mace; sweeten it with sugar; let it stand until it is but warm; then put in 1 quart of white wine; froth it up. To be eaten either with a spoon or the liquor may be pressed out to drink.

(For a twentieth-century family use $2\frac{1}{4}$ oz barley to 1 pint each of milk and single cream, and $\frac{1}{3}$ pint wine.)

❧ Beech ❧

Fagus sylvatica (Fagaceae)

The beech grows all over Britain but is indigenous only on the chalk and limestone of south-east England. The nuts of the tree (known as beech mast) are still valued on the continent as farm fodder but have only been used as human food in times of hardship – and there is no doubt that the collecting and peeling of the nuts is a time-consuming business. In America they have been ground for oil and meal and made into beech-nut butter and their use as a coffee substitute is quite widespread. (Meg Dods mentions this, and the use of roasted acorns, rye, 'pease' and beans in her Edinburgh cookery book of 1826.) But you don't need to be as particular as the American philosopher Thoreau in selecting your tree: 'I frequently tramped eight or ten miles through the deepest snow to keep an appointment with a beech-tree, or a yellow birch, or an old acquaintance among the pines' (Walden: *Winter Visitors*).

Not being a smoker, I have not been tempted to use the dried leaves as a tobacco substitute – this was tried with the German army during the First World War and, not surprisingly, proved a failure – but beech-leaf wine and noyau are well-tried favourites. 'The kernels or mast within are reported to ease the paine of the kidneyes proceeding of the stone, if they be eaten, and to cause the gravel and sand the easier to come forth. With these, Mice and Squirrels are greatly delighted, who do mightily increase by feeding thereon: Swine also be fatned herewith and certaine other beasts: also Deere do feed thereon very greedily: they be likewise pleasant to Thrushes and Pigeons' (Gerard). And John Evelyn writing in 1662 observes that 'in the cavities of these trees bees much delight to hive themselves'.

BEECH-NUT COFFEE

Peel the nuts and roast them in a hot oven until dry and brittle. Grind in an electric coffee grinder and prepare as coffee.

BEECH-LEAF NOYAU

Gather young clean leaves and pack them into a large Kilner jar, almost filling it. Cover with gin and leave to steep for a week or two. Strain off the gin (now a beautiful green) and add, for every pint of gin, syrup made with 6 oz of sugar and $\frac{1}{2}$ pint of water and a little brandy. Mix well and bottle when cold.

BEECH-LEAF WINE

1 gal beech leaves
$2\frac{3}{4}$ lb sugar
juice of 2 lemons
1 gal water
wine yeast and nutrient

Bring $\frac{1}{2}$ gal of the water to the boil and dissolve the sugar in it. Pour this over the leaves, infuse overnight and then strain into a fermenting vessel. Add lemon juice, nutrient and yeast, shake well, then top up with cold water to the bottom of the neck. Fit airlock and leave in a warm place to ferment. When clear, rack into a clean jar, and do this again before bottling.

❧ Bilberry ❧

Vaccinium myrtillus (Ericaceae)

A small wiry shrub growing densely on heaths and in mountain areas, especially in the north and west. The fruits are known as blaeberries in Scotland, whortleberries in parts of England and fraughans in Ireland, where Fraughan Sunday (the nearest to 1 August) has been revived as an excuse for general frivolity and an escape from the labour of picking them. It is a badge of several of the clans and, in a haunting Scottish song, the fairies steal a baby while the mother is gathering blaeberries. The leaves were used in the Highlands to adulterate tea and the small black flat-topped fruits for dyeing and for jams, tarts and syrups. Unfortunately the sheep eat the shrubs back before they can fruit, so look for them in sheep-free areas or grow them in your garden. They are also a favourite with the birds, whose droppings are stained with the seeds during the months of July and August.

BILBERRY-LEAF TEA

Carefully dry the young leaves and infuse as you would China tea, using about the same quantity of leaf.

BILBERRY LIQUEUR

This can be made in the same way as sloe gin (see under Blackthorn) and is every bit as good.

BILBERRY WINE

3 lb bilberries
3 lb sugar
yeast and nutrient
1 gal water
1 dessertspoon citric acid

Boil half the water and pour over the bilberries in a stone crock. Stir in the sugar and when the liquor is lukewarm add the rest of the water (cold), the acid, nutrient and yeast. Cover and ferment in a warm place for a few days, stirring well each day. Strain into a dark fermenting jar and fit an airlock. When clear, bottle and keep for at least six months before drinking, using dark bottles to keep the colour.

BILBERRY DRINK

Cook the berries in a little warm water with sugar to taste. Strain, add a dash of cinnamon or lemon, and drink hot. The fruit is astringent and this syrup is said to be useful in cases of diarrhoea.

❧ Birch ☙

Betula pendula (Betulaceae)

'The birch, most shy and ladylike of trees', (J. R. Lowell) thrives all over Europe in almost any situation. In Northumbria, fishermen used candles or torches of birch bark, and in the west of England birch crosses were hung over the doors of houses as a protection against evil. The leaves are very fragrant and in Finland are gathered into bunches and used in the sauna to beat and massage the skin. The combination of the smell of the hot pine of the sauna and the wet leaves is unforgettable. A Finnish ex-wartime pilot described to me how he used the leaves to relieve his rheumatism, which resulted from high-flying without adequate protection. Twice a year he would put on some old baggy clothes and stuff them with birch leaves. He would then secure the openings around ankles, wrists and neck and go to bed, asking to be wakened after three hours, by which time the leaves would be black with the heat generated – and the pain gone. Similar treatments have also been used in French country districts. In fact birch has been used medicinally for centuries: Culpeper mentions that the juice of the young leaves or the distilled sap was 'good to break the stone in the kidneys and bladder'. Here is Gerard on medicine of another sort: '... for in times past the magistrates roddes were made hereof: and in our time also the Schoolemasters and parents do terrifie their children with rods made of birch.' The birch is associated with the Buchanan clan, but they were never very terrifying.

Birch-Sap Wine 1

Tap the tree in early spring when the buds begin to swell but before they open into leaves. The sap at this time will be clear, but later it becomes thick and coloured. Choose a fairly large tree and bore a hole upwards at an angle of about 30 degrees to just beyond the bark where the sap rises. Insert a plastic tube that closely fits the hole and collect the sap in a well-secured bottle over several days. If the tree is very large you can tap it in several places; otherwise tap several trees in order to collect a sufficient quantity. Remember to plug the hole afterwards with a wooden plug. You can use the same holes the following year.

> 1 gal birch sap
> 2 lemons
> 1 sweet orange
> 1 lb raisins
> 3 lb sugar
> yeast and nutrient

Pare the orange and lemons with a sharp knife, avoiding the bitter white pith, and boil the peel in the sap for fifteen minutes. Make up to 1 gallon and pour into a crock containing the sugar and chopped raisins. Stir until the sugar is dissolved. When the liquor is lukewarm, add the fruit juice, yeast and nutrient and leave covered in a warm place until the fermentation is quieter. Strain into a fermenting jar and fit airlock. Leave for six months or so and then siphon off and bottle, using strong bottles, tying down the corks and storing them on their sides for a further six months. The taste reminds one of retsina.

Birch-Sap Wine 2
(Victorian recipe)

To every gallon of the sap add 1 pint of honey or 1 lb of sugar, stir the whole together, and boil it for an hour with a few cloves and a little lemon peel; at the same time carefully skim off the rising impurities. When cool a few spoonsful of new ale should be added to induce a proper degree of fermentation [use a wine yeast]; and after the yeast has settled, the wine should be bottled, corked tightly and kept for use. If this liquor be prepared with proper attention, it becomes so strong that the common stone bottles, into which it is decanted, frequently burst.

Birch-Leaf Tea

Make an infusion of the fresh or dried leaves and sweeten with honey. This is a pleasant aromatic drink and said to be good for rheumatism.

[21]

❧ Blackthorn ❧

Prunus spinosa (Rosaceae)

The surly blackthorn is a wanderer, a wood
that the artificer burns not;
Through his body, though it be scanty,
birds in their flocks warble.
(Old Irish: translated by S. O'Grady)

A common spiny shrub found in hedgerows, open woods and scrub throughout Britain: it is simply the wild plum, from which many of our cultivated species are derived. The flowers and fruit (sloes) have been used for centuries for medicinal purposes, the flowers being mildly purgative and the fruit 'binding'. Mixed with crab apples the latter makes a delicious attractive-looking jelly. We know that sloes have been enjoyed from prehistoric times: when the first-century BC village at Glastonbury lake was excavated, nearly a barrow-load of the stones was found.

Culpeper describes the sloe as 'when ripe, of a fine purplish black colour, of a sour austere taste, and not fit to be eaten until mellowed by frost'. This last is true, but you can still have sloe gin in time for Christmas. On a more sombre note, here is Gerard: 'The juice of sloes doth stop the belly, the lask and bloudy flix, the inordinat course of women's termes, and all other issues of bloud in man or woman.'

BLACKTHORN-LEAF TEA

Dry the young and tender leaves of the tree and make as you would China tea. You can also use the leaves fresh.

BLACKTHORN-FLOWER TEA
(Victorian recipe)

In a medicinal respect a handful of the flowers of the sloe tree, either infused in water or boiled in milk, and strained, affords a draught which operates as a safe and gentle purgative.

SLOE WINE

3 lb ripe sloes
$\frac{1}{2}$ lb raisins
$3\frac{1}{2}$ lb sugar
6 pints water
yeast and nutrient

Put the sloes in a stone crock and pour the boiling water over them. Mash the sloes well, add the chopped raisins, 2 lb of the sugar and, when lukewarm, the yeast and nutrient. Stir well, cover and leave to ferment for ten days, stirring daily. Strain, add the remaining sugar and pour into a fermenting jar. Fit an airlock and leave in a warm room for a month. If by this time the wine is too bitter, add sugar and leave to clear; then bottle and store for a year before drinking.

SLOE WHISKY

Put $\frac{1}{2}$ lb of sloes (pricked, as overleaf) into a Kilner jar with 6 oz of white sugar and 1 pint of whisky. Cover securely and shake daily for a month. Strain through muslin and bottle.

Sloe Gin

Half-fill a Kilner jar with clean, pricked sloes (prick the fruit with a darning needle to release the juice). Add $\frac{1}{2}$ lb of sugar for each $\frac{1}{2}$ lb of fruit and top up again with gin. Shake daily until the sugar is dissolved and, after that, occasionally for the next two months. Strain and bottle.

❧ Bog Myrtle ❧

Myrica gale (Myricaceae)

A deciduous bushy shrub, bog myrtle or sweet gale grows mainly on bogland. On the moors in summer the scent is almost over-powering, but at night-time there is no smell more refreshing. In the Highlands the leaves are still gathered and dried to scent linen and keep moths away, and it is said that a sweet-smelling wax for candles (the plant is known as candleberries in parts of England) is obtained by boiling the catkins in water. I suspect that this is a lot of work for a very small quantity. The bark has been used to dye wool yellow, the dried berries for flavouring broths, and the leaves are still used as a substitute for hops, for which purpose they dry very successfully. In Sweden in 1440 King Christopher confirmed an old law which rendered punishable by fine the offence of cutting or injuring the sweet gale, or collecting it on any other person's land, or gathering it on a common before a stated day.

Gerard says the fruit 'is troublesome to the brain; being put into beere or aile whilst it is in boiling, it maketh the same heady, fit to make a man quickly drunk'. In my experience beer made with bog myrtle alone is not quite as strong as that made with hops; but it is clean and refreshing and still quite strong enough. 'It is tried by experience that it is good to be put in beare both by me and by diverse other in Summersetshyre' (Turner: *A New Herball*, 1551). In Denmark today you can buy a bottle of aquavit in which the herb is steeped.

Bog Myrtle or Gale Beer

- 10 oz malt etrxact
- 8 oz sugar
- 1 dessertspoon dried yeast
- 1 gal water
- 1 oz dried bog myrtle (a little more if using it fresh)

Boil the bog myrtle in the water for several minutes. Strain on to the malt and sugar in a stone jar. Stir well till dissolved and, when lukewarm, sprinkle on the yeast. Cover with a cloth and leave in a warm place to ferment for five or six days. Siphon the beer off the sediment and bottle in screw-top bottles, adding 1 teaspoon of sugar to each bottle. Leave for at least a week before drinking.

Mulled Ale
(See also under Hops)

Heat a pint of beer with sugar to taste (say, 2 oz), add a small piece of cinnamon stick and

[23]

a grating of nutmeg. Do not boil, but strain and serve hot.

MULLED ALE
(Victorian recipe)

Heat a quart of ale with sugar and any spice, according to taste; add wine, brandy, rum or butter to your taste, and serve it with toast.

ALE POSSET
(Victorian recipe)

Take a small piece of white bread; put it into a pint of ale made hot in a saucepan; when soft, take it off the fire and grate in half a nutmeg. Put in sugar to your taste; then pour it into a china bowl, and put in by degrees a pint of white wine. Serve it with toast on a plate.

❧ Borage ❧

Borago officinalis (Boraginaceae)

Borage is an introduced annual which has naturalised in waste places throughout Britain. It is well worth growing in the garden as it is a handsome and useful plant and, although an annual, it readily seeds itself and will come up in the same plot year after year. It used to be very common, grown for its leaves and roots as well as for its pretty blue star-like flowers. The flowers were candied, or steeped in wine together with the cucumber-scented leaves.

In Italy I found borage growing wild in the mountains and flowering right through the winter. The village women there cook it like spinach and add it to the flour and egg mixture when making pasta, to which it gives a good flavour as well as an attractive green colour. Bees love the plant, possibly because they see best at the blue end of the spectrum, and they will work it even in the rain. The honey is excellent.

The old herbalists recommended borage for melancholy and 'to comfort the heart and spirits'. There is an old rhyme which goes:

Ego Borago   I, Borage
Gaudia semper ago. Bring aluaies courage.

Indeed the name borage comes from a corruption of the Latin *cor* (the heart) and *ago* (I bring) and one of its Welsh names is *Llawenlys* (herb of gladness). 'The leaf of burrage,' says Bacon, 'hath an excellent spirit to repress the fuliginous vapour of dusky melancholia.'

BORAGE TEA
(leaf or flower)

Pick unblemished leaves and flowers and dry separately on sheets of paper in a shady place. Make tea in the usual way, using 1 teaspoon of either dried leaves or flowers per cup. Infuse for a few minutes, strain and sweeten with honey. You can also use fresh leaves, but you will need rather more per cup.

SUMMER WINE CUP

Steep fresh borage in a little water until it has imparted its faint cucumber flavour. Strain, mix with sugar, add white wine and a slice or two of lemon. Decorate with borage flowers and young leaves.

[24]

Bramble

Rubus fructicosus (Rosaceae)

'It is so well known that it needeth no description,' says Culpeper, and indeed most of us have at one time or another been pretty intimately entangled with a bramble bush. Its binding qualities probably account for the curious English rituals in which children suffering from hernias or ruptures were passed or dragged in and out of a loop of bramble which had been rooted at either end. Similarly, in Cornwall, dragging or creeping under a bramble arch was a charm against boils and rheumatism.

The leaf and fruit have many virtues. 'The leaves of the Bramble boiled in water, with honey, allum, and a little white wine added thereto, make a most excellent lotion or washing water to heale the sores in the mouth, the privie parts of man or woman, and the same decoction fastneth the teeth' (Gerard). Nowadays, blackberry jams and syrups are used for bronchial catarrh and sore throats, blackberry vinegar for feverish colds and a decoction of the dried leaves boiled in water for dysentery and diarrhoea.

BRAMBLE-LEAF TEA

Dry the leaves carefully and use 1 oz to 1 pint of water. Infuse as usual and drink cold as a remedy for 'summer complaint'. Sweeten with honey for sore throats and thrush. Try also mixing with woodruff leaves and, of course, you can use the leaves fresh.

BRAMBLE CORDIAL

Boil the berries until they break up, and strain through a bag. To each pint of juice add 1 lb of sugar, $\frac{1}{2}$ oz of mace and 2 teaspoons of cloves (whole, not ground). Stir over a gentle flame until the sugar is dissolved and boil for a minute or two. When cool, strain and add $\frac{3}{4}$ cup of whisky to each quart of juice. Bottle and seal.

BRAMBLE-TIP WINE

1 gal bramble tips
3 lb sugar
1 teaspoon citric acid
1 gal water
wine yeast and nutrient

Place the tips in a crock and cover with boiling water. Leave to stand overnight then bring to the boil and simmer for fifteen minutes. Strain through muslin on to the sugar and when lukewarm add the nutrient and yeast. Keep covered in a warm place for ten days, then pour into a fermenting jar and fit airlock. When clear, siphon off and bottle.

BRAMBLE SYRUP

Press the berries to obtain the juice and cook equal quantities of the juice and sugar to a syrupy consistency. Bottle and use for sore throats and bronchial catarrh, or diluted in water as a refreshing drink.

BRAMBLE WINE

5 lb brambles
$2\frac{1}{4}$ lb sugar
1 gal water
wine yeast and nutrient

Pick the fruit on a fine day, place in a crock

and crush with a wooden spoon. Pour the boiling water over the crushed fruit, stir well and, when lukewarm, add the yeast and nutrient. Cover and leave for four or five days, stirring daily. Strain through muslin on to the sugar, stirring well to dissolve. Pour into a dark fermentation vessel, but only to the shoulder.

Fit an airlock and keep spare liquor in a smaller bottle with a cotton-wool plug. When fermentation quietens after a week or so, top up with the spare wine and refit the airlock. Leave until clear, rack and later bottle in dark bottles so as to preserve the attractive colour of the wine.

❧ Broom ❧

Sarothamnus scoparius (Papilionaceae)

From the number of broom place-names in Britain, e.g. Bromley, Brompton, it appears that broom was once more widespread than it is now; but it is still fairly common on sandy pastures, heaths and open woodlands, and is also frequently cultivated in gardens, there being many beautiful varieties. Most of us know a song or ballad which features the broom and it is also known as an heraldic device, its mediaeval name – *Planta genista* – having given the family name of Plantaganet to the line of Henry II of England. He wore it in his cap – and you can find a broom plant with its open pods (the seeds scattered) on the robe of Richard II on his tomb in Westminster Abbey.

Before the introduction of hops, the tender green tops of broom were used to flavour beer and to make it more intoxicating, and farmers have noticed that sheep become briefly intoxicated on the pods. The flower buds (just before they begin to show yellow) used to be pickled in imitation of capers, and a tea made with the flowers is still an approved diuretic. 'That worthy Prince of famous memorie Henry VIII, King of England, was woont to drink the distilled water of Broome floures against surfets and diseases thereof arising' (Gerard).

BROOM TONIC

1 oz broom tops
½ oz dandelion roots
½ oz bruised juniper berries
pinch of cayenne

Boil broom and dandelion in 1 pint of water until reduced by half, adding the juniper berries towards the end. Strain when cool, add a pinch of cayenne, and take a wineglass three or four times a day.

BROOM COFFEE

Gather a large quantity of ripe broom pods and set your friends and family to the laborious task of removing the seeds. Roast them in a hot oven, making sure they do not burn, and grind them in a marble mortar. Make coffee with them in the usual way. M. Pagot des Charmes says this makes an excellent coffee but, having lived in the nineteenth century, he is beyond the vengeance of your family and friends if they think it not worth the effort.

Spartium Scoparium

BROOM

Broom Wine

1 gal broom flowers
1 gal water
3 lb white sugar
2 oranges, 2 lemons
wine yeast and nutrient

Pare the oranges and lemons with a sharp knife, leaving out all the bitter white pith, and boil the rinds in the water with the sugar. When it is lukewarm pour it over the flowers, add the orange and lemon juice, the nutrient and the yeast. Stand in a warm place (covered) for two days, then strain into a fermentation jar and fit an airlock. Leave to ferment, rack and, when clear, bottle.

❧ Catmint ☙

Nepata cataria (Labiatae)

Catmint (or catnep), which belongs to the same large family as the mints and dead nettles, is a native perennial growing wild in south and east England in hedgerows, on dry banks and by the edges of fields. It is much less common farther north but is often and easily grown in gardens, not requiring the same moisture as the other mints. It makes a pretty border when it hasn't been flattened by cats rolling in it — a point to be remembered when picking this plant !

Catnep tea is very pleasant and is supposed to be useful in cases of fever and the common cold, inducing sleep and perspiration without over-heating the system. Gerard's suggestion sounds refreshing enough too, but I can't say I've tried it : 'It is used in baths and decoctions for women to sit over, to bring down their sicknesse, and to make them fruitfull.'

a little honey. The leaves can be combined with peppermint and chamomile for an excellent tea.

Catnep Tea

Pour 1 pint of boiling water over a $\frac{1}{2}$ cup of broken leaves and stems. Allow to stand for several minutes, then strain and sweeten with

❧ Chamomile ❧

Anthemis nobilis; Matricaria chamomilla; Matricaria matricarioides (Compositae)

The first is a perennial, sweetly aromatic and found on sandy soil in the south of England and south-west Ireland. The others are annuals, *M. matricarioides* (an alien) having greenish flower heads and no rays. This one is the most common and was also called *Chamaemelum nudum odoratum* – sweet naked chamomile. It is found in waste places and on farm tracks ('Like a chamomile bed, the more it is trodden the more it will spread').

Chamomile tea is given to children when they are teething, or to prevent nightmares, as it has a harmless sedative effect. The flowers are also recommended for their tonic properties, besides being used by blondes as a hair rinse. Gerard, who seems to claim more knowledge of midwifery than was proper for a sixteenth-century gentleman, writes that a decoction made in white wine 'expelleth the dead child, and secondine or afterbirth, speedily, and clenseth those parts'.

CHAMOMILE TEA

Pour 2 pints of boiling water on $\frac{1}{2}$ oz of dried chamomile flowers and let stand for five minutes, or use the flowers fresh. Sweeten with honey and add a slice of lemon if you like.

HIGHLAND BITTERS

In Scotland bitters were traditionally drunk before meals, especially breakfast, 'for the purpose of strenthening the stomache, and by that means invigorating the general health'. Any kind of spirit could be used and sometimes wine or ale.

> $1\frac{3}{4}$ oz gentian root
> 1 oz coriander seed
> $\frac{1}{2}$ oz bitter orange peel
> $\frac{1}{4}$ oz chamomile flowers
> $\frac{1}{2}$ oz cloves (whole)
> $\frac{1}{2}$ oz cinnamon stick
> 2 bottles whisky

Finely chop the gentian root and orange peel (free of pith). Place in mortar with seeds, cloves, cinnamon and chamomile flowers. Bruise all together, place in an earthenware jar, pour in the whisky and make the jar air-tight. Leave for ten days, then strain and bottle.

You will be lucky if you are able to buy gentian root at your local chemist, but *Gentiana lutea* is well worth growing in the garden, quite apart from its medicinal value; and our own native felworts 'have been proved not to be a whit inferior in virtue to that which comes from beyond the sea' (Culpeper).

CHAMOMILE TONIC
(French recipe)

Macerate the following for ten days in a bottle of good wine: 1 oz of chamomile flowers, a piece of orange or lemon peel (free from pith) and 10 large sugar lumps. Strain and drink a wine-glassful before meals.

Matricaria Chamomilla

Chamomile

❧ Cherry ❧

Prunus avium; Prunus cerasus (Rosaceae)

Called gean in the North Country and in Scotland (from the French *guigne*), *Prunus avium* is a small native tree. It is fairly common in woods and hedgerows, and very pretty with its white blossoms in springtime. The wood is valued by craftsmen, and the fruits can be used in the same ways as the larger cultivated varieties – for wines, jellies, tarts and liqueurs. *Prunus cerasus*, the wild morello cherry, is smaller and, though not a native, is found now and again in hedges. This is the one favoured by Gerard: 'The common blacke cherries do strengthen the stomack, and are wholesomer than the red cherries, the which being dried do stop the lask.'

GEAN WHISKY

4 lb cherries
4 cherry kernels
1 bitter almond
1 blade mace
2 peppercorns
1 lb sugar
1 quart whisky
nutmeg

Stalk and stone the fruit, then bruise them and put them in a jar. Crack the kernels and add these, with the sugar and spices, to the jar. Pour over the whisky, cover and stir daily for a week, then seal and cork. Leave for a year before straining and bottling.

CHERRY RATAFIA
(Victorian recipe)

Take the stalks from the quantity of cherries you intend to use, and put a few raspberries with them; bruise and put them into a jar, and let them stand for four or five days, stirring the pulp two or three times a day; then press out all the juice, measure it, and to every 3 pints of it put 1 quart of brandy; add to these 5 pints [i.e. 3 pints of juice plus 2 pints of brandy] 3 handsful of kernels pounded, and $1\frac{1}{4}$ lb of sugar. Infuse in the same jar a handful of coriander and a little cinnamon. Let it stand seven or eight days, stirring it every day; then filter it, put it into bottles, and cork well.

CHERRY BRANDY OR WHISKY
(Meg Dods)

Pick morello or black cherries from the stalks, and drop them into bottles until the bottles are three-quarters full; top up with brandy or whisky. In three weeks, strain off the spirits and season with cinnamon and clove mixture, adding syrup to taste.

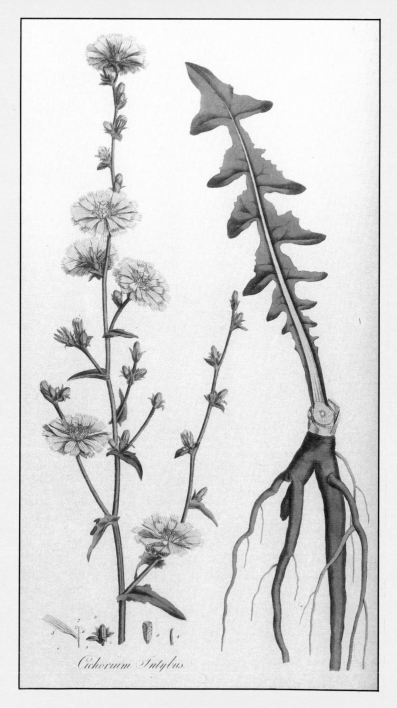

Cichorium Intybus.

CHICORY

❧ Chicory ❧

Cichorium intybus (Compositae)

Wild chicory grows in many parts of England and Ireland – especially in the southern counties – in waste places, by roadsides and on field edges. It is a hardy perennial and will grow in almost any soil. On the continent it is grown not only as a vegetable and salad, but also for fodder and for the root which is roasted, ground and used as an addition to or as a substitute for coffee. For this purpose it is best to collect the seed or buy some and sow it in May in the garden; treat it as you would carrots to produce fleshier roots than you would find in the wild.

To obtain the delicious blanched heads you buy in the shops as a salad, dig up the roots in October, cut off the green parts (except for a short length) and, after leaving them exposed to the air for two or three weeks, plant them in deep boxes filled with light sandy soil. Cover the boxes to keep out the light and put them in a warm cellar or greenhouse. Deprived of light in this way, the plants will yield soft creamy-white pointed heads with only a hint of the bitterness of the open-air leaves.

CHICORY COFFEE

Dig some of the long tap-roots, scrub them thoroughly and roast them slowly in an oven until they are hard and brittle, showing dark brown on the inside. Then grind and brew as you would coffee, remembering that chicory is somewhat stronger than coffee, so less should be used.

❧ Clover ❧

Trifolium pratense; Trifolium repens (Papilionaceae)

Red clover is very common all over the British Isles, especially in light sandy meadows where it flowers profusely and makes excellent hay. Gerard calls it a three-leafed grass or trefoil. As children we used to pull apart the flowers and suck out the nectar though, curiously, the bees prefer the white variety. Clover is so rich that animals have to be accustomed to it.

TAMORA: *I will enchant the old Andronicus,—*
With words more sweet and yet more
dangerous,

Than baits to fish, or honey-stalks to sheep;
When as the one is wounded with the bait,
The other rotted with delicious feed.
(Shakespeare: *Titus Andronicus*, IV, 4)

The flowers can be used in spring salads or brewed into tea. In the Appalachians this was known as 'spring bracer', and with honey added it made a good tea that was also a tonic. Clover blossoms were often combined with mints in midsummer or used in 'old field tea' made of sage, mullein, clover blossoms and

Trifolium repens.

CLOVER

basswood blooms (lime blossom). The flowers can also be combined with apples to make a pleasant-tasting jelly, or an excellent wine.

CLOVER TEA

Pour 1 pint of boiling water over 1 oz of the flowers. Let stand for a few minutes and drink sweetened with a little honey. With or without honey, this tea is rather cloying for some tastes, but you can try adding a small amount of dried spearmint or peppermint leaves.

CLOVER WINE

2 quarts red clover flowers
3 lb white sugar
2 oranges
3 lemons
1 gal water
wine yeast and nutrient

Gather the flowers on a dry day. Remove the stalks, put them into a crock and pour over them the boiling water. Meanwhile pare the oranges and lemons and add the rind (without any pith) and the sugar to the liquor. When lukewarm add the fruit juice, yeast and nutrient. Leave for five days, stirring regularly. Strain into a fermentation jar, fit an airlock and, when fermentation has ceased and the wine is clear, siphon off into bottles and leave for at least six months.

❧ Currant ❧

Ribes nigrum (blackcurrant); *Ribes rubrum* (redcurrant) *(Grossulariaceae)*

The blackcurrant is a native of Britain and northern Europe and is occasionally found wild by streams and in damp woods. It was probably used in folk-medicine long before it was introduced into gardens. It grows well in most situations and the main difficulty is in protecting the fruit from the birds. Good netting is essential.

The leaves have a strong distinctive aroma and when dry make a good tea, either by themselves or mixed with Indian tea. Gerard describes the fruit as being 'of a stinking and somewhat loathing savour', but it is now popular enough to be commercially viable as a good source of vitamin C. The redcurrant is also a hardy native and cultivation has given us a white variety. Redcurrant jelly is delicious served with lamb or game, as an ingredient of sauces (e.g. Cumberland sauce) and of desserts, and the juice is a pleasant acid in punch.

You can boil the juice of either currant to an extract with sugar – this is called a rob and is good for sore throats (try adding some to gin!). A soothing drink is also made simply by dissolving a tablespoonful of blackcurrant jam or jelly in a glass of boiling water, and the berries can be put in brandy, as you would black cherries, to make a delicious liqueur.

BLACKCURRANT TEA

Dry the young leaves carefully and use as you would China tea, or add a few to your usual brew – or use fresh leaves in a slightly larger quantity.

[35]

Currant Water
(Victorian recipe)

Pick $1\frac{1}{2}$ lb of currants and $\frac{1}{2}$ lb of raspberries, both quite ripe; crush them, press the juice through a sieve, and put to it a quart of water and $\frac{3}{4}$ lb of sugar; let it stand half an hour; then pass it through a napkin, pour it into decanters and set them in iced water.

Blackcurrant or Redcurrant Wine

> 3 lb blackcurrants (or redcurrants)
> 3 lb sugar
> 1 gal water
> wine yeast and nutrient

Crush the fruit in an earthenware crock. Boil the sugar in the water and pour on to the currants. When lukewarm, add the yeast and nutrient; cover and leave in a warm place for five days, stirring daily. Strain into a dark fermentation jar, fit an airlock and leave until fermentation ceases and the wine is clear. Siphon off into dark bottles to keep the colour.

Highland Cordial

> 1 pint whitecurrants
> 1 lb loaf sugar
> 1 lemon
> 1 teaspoon essence of ginger
> 1 bottle whisky

Strip the currants off the stalks. Peel the lemon thinly, discarding all the bitter white pith. Put the currants, lemon rind and ginger essence into a large Kilner jar and pour the whisky over them. Mix and cover so that it is air-tight, and leave for forty-eight hours. Strain, add the sugar and shake daily until it is dissolved. Bottle, cork and leave for three months before drinking.

Currant Shrub
(Meg Dods)

White or red is made by putting the juice of the fruit to rum or brandy, in the proportions of a pint of juice, or less, to a quart of spirit, and adding sugar to taste. It must then be filtered.

❦ Dandelion ❧

Taraxacum officinale (Compositae)

No one seems to know how the dandelion got its name – *dent de lion* in French, *dens leonis* in mediaeval Latin – but various theories have been put forward. Some say it is the jagged leaf which resembles the lion's teeth, others the white root; others believe its name refers to the golden teeth of the heraldic lion. The popular name, piss-a-bed, is equally widespread – *pissenlit* in France – and this obviously refers to the dandelion's diuretic qualities.

It is a useful bee plant, flowering in the cold days of spring right through to late autumn, and providing good supplies of pollen and nectar. The young leaves are delicious as a salad – blanched, they are almost equal to endive. They can also be cooked like spinach or made into broth, and in some parts of the country they are mixed with other herbs and

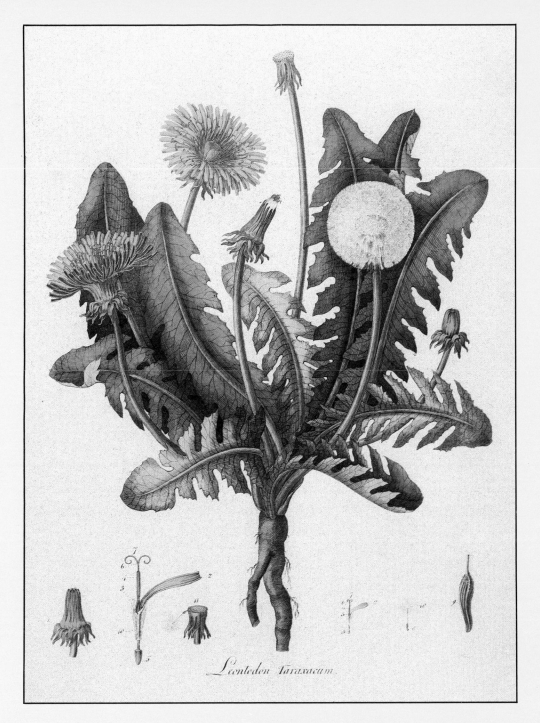

Leontodon Taraxacum.

Dandelion

made into tonic beers. The flowers too are made into wines and the roasted roots are ground and used like coffee, or mixed with it. For this purpose you need large well-formed roots, so it might well be worth your while cultivating the plants if you have the space. Medicinally the dandelion has been considered useful for liver complaints, for 'stone and gravel', and as a spring tonic.

'You see here what virtues this common herb hath and that is the reson the French and the Dutch so often eat them in spring; and now if you look a little farther, you may see plainly without a pair of spectacles, that foreign physicians are not so selfish as ours are, but more communicative of the virtues of plants to people' (Culpeper).

DANDELION TEA

Infuse 1 oz of dandelion in 1 pint of boiling water for ten minutes; decant, sweeten with honey, and drink several times a day as a tonic.

DANDELION COFFEE

Wash sizeable dandelion roots, peel them and roast until they are dark brown inside and will break with a snap. Grind and use as a coffee substitute or mixed with real coffee. The roots should be dug up in autumn, washed, cut in pieces and dried in the sun. In this state they will keep for years and can be roasted when required. (Ground dandelion root was sometimes mixed with chocolate.)

DANDELION BEER

½ lb young dandelion plants
1 gal water
1 lb brown sugar
1 lemon
½ oz root ginger
1 oz cream of tartar
1 oz yeast

Wash the plants and remove hairs from the main tap-root. Boil them with the bruised ginger and the lemon rind (having discarded the pith) for ten minutes. Strain on to the sugar and cream of tartar in an earthenware jar and stir until dissolved. When lukewarm add the lemon juice and yeast, cover the jar, and leave in a warm place for three days. Siphon off into screw-top bottles and leave for a week before drinking.

DANDELION WINE

2 quarts dandelions
3 lb sugar
4 oranges
1 gal water
wine yeast and nutrient

Pick the flowers in sunshine when they are fully opened, and make the wine immediately. Pour the boiling water over the flowers and leave to steep for two days (no longer). Boil the mixture for ten minutes with the orange peel (discard any pith) and strain through muslin on to the sugar, stirring until it is dissolved. When lukewarm, add the fruit juice, yeast and nutrient. Put into a fermentation jar, fit an airlock and leave until fermentation has ceased and the wine has cleared. Siphon off and bottle.

❧ Elder ❧

Sambucus nigra (Caprifoliaceae)

Bour-tree — Bour-tree: crooked rong
Never straight and never strong;
Ever bush and never tree
Since our Lord was nailed on thee.

Traditionally the elder is either the tree on which Judas hanged himself, or the tree of the cross of Calvary, being supposed to be stunted and twisted ever since. Twisted it may be, but for us it is a symbol of merriment, not grief, as it produces two of the very best country wines, and the 'stink' (Shakespeare calls it the 'stinking elder') is not unpleasant and is supposed to keep off the flies — it used to be stuck in the bridles of horses for that purpose. Country people are often reluctant to cut down, prune or burn the tree for fear of ill-luck; and throughout northern Europe (especially Denmark) the tree is associated with magic. It was supposed to ward off witches and evil influences and this probably accounts for the numerous trees and bushes one finds planted round old cottages.

In July and August elders are a familiar and lovely sight — masses of creamy blossoms with all the fragrance of summer. And the uses are endless. When the pith is pushed out of the young stems you can make a whistle or pop-gun or bellows, and the white close-grained wood of the old trees is suitable for many small polished articles, instruments and toys.

Gardeners have boiled the leaves in water and used the resulting liquid to keep their plants free from caterpillars; in some places an infusion of the leaves is applied to the skin as an insect repellent. In the Hebrides the root and leaves were used to dye wool black; with alum, green; and the berries to dye blue and purple.

The medicinal properties of all parts of the plant are equally varied and bark, leaves and flowers are made into drinks, ointments, eye-lotions and poultices. Elderberry wine and elderberry tea are well-known remedies for colds and 'flu. The wine resembles port, and indeed it was found that the medicinal virtues of old red port in the late nineteenth century could be traced to the elderberry with which it was commonly adulterated.

On a cold winter's night elderberry wine makes a marvellous drink when mulled with a little sugar, some spices and a slice or two of orange; and the syrups and robs are very pleasant and equally effective. It is well worth while growing a few elders in your garden. They are hardy, like moisture and shade and will provide a good and compact hedge if regularly clipped.

ELDERFLOWER TEA

Use 2 teaspoonsful of dried elderflowers per cup, pour boiling water over the flowers in a china teapot, infuse for a few minutes, then strain and sweeten with honey to taste.

ELDER ELECTUARY
(Victorian recipe)

Take 5 lb of the juice of elderberries and 1 lb of good brown sugar or honey. Let them simmer gently till like thick syrup, and take a spoonful mixed with a little water at bedtime. This preparation is good for a cough, and keeps well.

[39]

ELDER SYRUP
(Victorian recipe)

Pick the berries from the stalks, and put them in an earthenware pot, with ½ pint of water to each quart of berries, cover them, and set them in an oven until they are sufficiently stewed to extract the juice from them. To every pint of syrup add 1 lb of brown sugar and a little bruised ginger; boil half an hour, and when cold bottle it, cork it up closely, and keep it in a cool place. When to be taken warm at bed-time, as in cases of cold or sore throat, boil a little grated nutmeg or lemon-peel in water a few minutes, and then add one-third of the syrup to two-thirds of water, and a little lemon juice. Blackberry syrup may be prepared in the same way.

ELDERFLOWER 'CHAMPAGNE'
(Non-alcoholic)

3 large heads of elder flowers
1½ lb sugar
1 gal water (spring water if available)
1 lemon
2 tablespoons white wine vinegar

Gather the flowers when they are in full bloom. Trim them from their stems with scissors, place them in a crock, add the juice and the thinly peeled rind of the lemon (avoid the pith), the sugar and the vinegar. Pour over 1 gallon of cold water and steep for forty-eight hours. Strain into strong screw-top bottles and leave for a fortnight, by which time it should be highly effervescent.

ELDERFLOWER WINE

1 pint elderflowers
1 gal water
2½ lb sugar
½ lb raisins

juice of 3 lemons
wine yeast and nutrient

Trim the flowers from the stems with scissors. Put sugar, flowers, raisins and lemon juice in a crock. Pour on boiling water, stir well and allow to cool to lukewarm. Add wine yeast and nutrient. Cover closely and leave in a warm place for five days, stirring daily. Strain through muslin into a fermentation vessel, fit an airlock and leave to ferment. Siphon off when clear into a clean jar and bottle when fermentation has ceased — which may be well over six months later.

ELDERFLOWER 'CHAMPAGNE'
(Alcoholic)

Proceed exactly as above but bottle in Champagne-type bottles shortly before fermen-tation seems likely to cease. Wire down the corks.

ELDERBERRY WINE

3 lb elderberries
3 lb sugar
1 gal water
wine yeast and nutrient

Strip the berries from the stalks with a fork, weigh them, and crush them in a crock. Pour on the boiling water and let cool to lukewarm before adding the yeast and nutrient. Leave three days, stirring daily, then strain through muslin on to the sugar. Pour the liquor into a dark fermentation vessel (so that the wine keeps its colour) but reserve some in a separate bottle until the first vigorous fermentation has subsided, plugging the necks with cotton wool. When quieter, top up and fit an airlock. When fermentation has ceased and the wine is clear, siphon off into dark bottles and keep for at least six months.

❧ Fennel ❧

Foeniculum vulgare (Umbelliferae)

Mirie it is, in time of June,
When Fenil hangith abrode in toun.

Fennel is a hardy perennial which grows wild on chalky cliffs in the south of England, and in Ireland, but it will also do well in most places when sown in the garden. It is a handsome plant with bright green feathery leaves and golden flowers which has been cultivated since Roman times for its edible shoots and seeds. The old herbalists recommended it for strengthening the sight, but it was also used in the Middle Ages to ward off evil spirits. Its origins as a seasoning are in Italy and as such it has long been associated with fish, especially the salt fish of Lent.

'... Both the seeds and root of our garden Fennel are much used in drinks and broths for those that are grown fat, to abate their unwieldiness and cause them to grow more gaunt and lean,' wrote William Coles (*Nature's Paradise*, 1650); and there are other references to this property, to fennel's power to aid longevity, to give strength and courage and, at a baser level, as a carminative – gripe water contains fennel and dill waters. Gerard writes: 'The greene leaves of Fennell eaten, or the seed drunken made into a ptisan, do fill women's breasts with milke.'

Fennel Water
(Victorian recipe)

This is done simply by steeping some fennel in hot water till it has the taste of the herb sufficiently; add what sugar you think proper, and keep it in a cool place a good while before using. You may ice it or not, according as you may think proper.

Fennel Tea

Pour $\frac{1}{2}$ pint of boiling water on a teaspoonful of bruised fennel seeds. (Formerly also used as a carminative.)

❧ Flag Iris ❧

Iris pseudacorus (Iridaceae)

A very beautiful stately plant growing in watery places throughout the British Isles – by lochs, rivers, ponds and ditches. Culpeper calls it 'myrtle flag' or 'myrtle grass' and it is also called *fleur de lys*, being the heraldic emblem of the kings of France and a familiar feature in French tapestry. Formerly the rhizome was used as a powerful cathartic but, being very acrid, it is rarely used now. Gerard mentions another interesting use for it: 'The root, boiled soft, with a few drops of water upon it, laid plaisterwise upon the face of man or woman, doth in two daies at the most take away the blacknesse and blewnesse of any stroke or bruise.' He also recommends that a piece of silk be laid between the 'plaister' and the skin if the latter is delicate or tender.

The flowers have been used in Scotland to give a yellow dye and the root with iron sulphate to give a good black, which was employed in ink-making. It was a French chemist in the early nineteenth century who discovered that the roasted seeds made an acceptable substitute for coffee, even asserting that they were superior in flavour. This used to be called Sylvester's coffee.

FLAG IRIS COFFEE

Collect the ripe fruits of the yellow flag in late summer and free the seeds from the pods. Roast well and grind and prepare as for ordinary coffee.

❧ Gooseberry ❧

Ribes uva-crispa (Grossulariaceae)

The gooseberry bush was a familiar sight in gardens by Culpeper's time, though it is, like the blackcurrant and redcurrant, a native of the British Isles, growing wild in woods and hedges. Gooseberry sauce has long been an accompaniment to mackerel – the French word for gooseberry being *groseille à maquerau* (literally, 'mackerel currant'). The fruit is a favourite for fools, tarts, chutneys, jams and wine. 'They provoke the appetite, and coole the vehement heate of the stomache and liver,' says Gerard – and an infusion of the dried leaves was used more recently as a tonic for adolescent girls.

BEST WHITE GOOSEBERRY CHAMPAGNE
(Meg Dods)

To every Scotch pint (=2 quarts) of white gooseberries mashed, add $1\frac{1}{2}$ quarts of water,

Iris Pseudacorus.

FLAG IRIS

and 12 ounces of good loaf-sugar bruised and dissolved. Stir the whole well in the tub or vat, and throw a blanket over the vessel; which is proper in making all wines, unless you wish to slacken the process of fermentation. Stir the ingredients occasionally; and in three days strain off the liquor into a cask. Keep the cask full, and when the spiritous fermentation has ceased, add for every gallon of wine ½ pint of brandy or good whisky, and the same quantity of Sherry or Madeira. Bung up the cask very closely, covering the bung with clay; and when fined, which will be in from three to six months, rack it carefully off.

GOOSEBERRY WINE

4 lb ripe red gooseberries
3 lb sugar
1 gal water
yeast and nutrient

Top and tail the fruit, mash well in a stone crock, then add the cold water and the yeast and nutrient. Stand for three days, stirring twice a day. Strain through muslin and dissolve the sugar in the juice. Put into a fermentation jar, fit an airlock and leave until fermentation has ceased and the wine is clear. Siphon off into bottles and cork.

❧ Goosegrass ❧

Galium aparine (Rubiaceae)

Cleavers, or sticky-willy as I knew it as a child, belongs to the same order as the bed-straws, sweet woodruff and the coffee tree (*Coffea arabica*) and so it comes as no surprise that the ripe seeds can be roasted and ground as a coffee substitute – and in the past have been used as such, in Sweden in particular.

In the garden it is a nuisance, but it is still valued by herbalists for its medicinal action. The juice is given for skin disorders, such as psoriasis, and it is a powerful diuretic. Cleavers tea is recommended for insomnia and for colds, and Culpeper recommended it for obesity, as did Gerard before him:

'Women do usually make pottage of Clevers with a little mutton and otemeale to cause lanknesse and keep them from fatnesse.'
Cleavers was formerly used for a red dye (Isle of Jura) and people say that the bones of poultry feeding on the roots acquire a red colour. The whole plant is eaten by most animals, but is especially enjoyed by young geese – hence the name.

CLEAVERS TEA

Dry the leaves carefully and use 1 oz infused in a pint of boiling water. This is soothing and induces restful sleep, and used also to be a rural remedy for colds.

GOOSEGRASS COFFEE

Dry the seeds, roast for a few minutes in a hot oven, grind and prepare as you would coffee.

Galium Aparine

Goosegrass

❧ Gorse ❧

Ulex europaeus (Papilionaceae)

When gorse is out of bloom,
Kissing's out of season

— but of course gorse is found blooming, here and there, throughout the year. It is not so important medicinally as broom, which it resembles, nor is it such a useful plant, but it has been used quite extensively as fuel and the ashes even mixed with clay and used as a substitute for soap. In some parts of England the bushes were crushed in a mill and then used as a fodder for horses and cows, the latter yielding good milk on this food alone.

Gorse makes a good hedge when closely cut and does well in a mild climate and by the sea. 'The Furze bush is a plant altogether a-Thorne, fully armed with most sharpe prickles, without any leaves at all except in the Spring' (Gerard). It is still known as furze in the south-west — whin is more common in Scotland and in the north and east of England. From Yorkshire comes the grim 'Lyke Wake Dirge':

When thou from hence away art past,
Every nighte and alle,
To whinny-muir thou com'st at last;
And Christ receive thy saule.

If ever thou gavest hosen and shoon,
Every nighte and alle,
Sit thee down and put them on;
And Christ receive thy saule.

If hosen and shoon thou ne'er gav'st nane,
Every nighte and alle,
The whinnies shall prick thee to the bare bane;
And Christ receive thy saule . . .

GORSE WINE

1 gal gorse flowers
2½ lb sugar
2 oranges
2 lemons
1 gal water
yeast and nutrient

Boil the flowers in the water for fifteen minutes, then strain through a flannel bag and add water to make up the original 1 gallon. Dissolve the sugar in the liquid and add the lemon and orange peel (free of pith) and the juice. When lukewarm add the yeast and nutrient. Leave for three days in a warm place, stirring occasionally, then strain into a fermenting jar, fit an air-lock and leave until fermentation has ceased and wine is clear. Siphon off into bottles and cork.

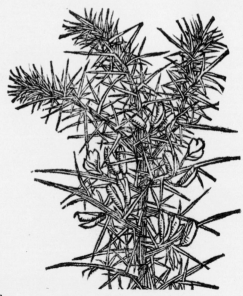

Glechoma hederacea

GROUND IVY

❧ Ground Ivy ❧

Glechoma hederacea (Labiatae)

This is a common plant of hedge banks and waste places. The leaves somewhat resemble ivy and it has small violet-blue flowers. Like woodsage, it was used as a bitter in the brewing of beer before the widespread use of hops – hence one of its popular names, alehoof. No doubt for this reason and for its other medicinal properties, it was taken over to New England, and my recipes for ground ivy tea come from America. In England, however, Anne Pratt (writing in 1857) mentions that 'the leaves are much used in villages to make an infusion for coughs' and that 'even in recent times a quantity of this plant has been thrown into a vat of ale in order to clarify it, and the ale thus prepared has been taken as a remedy for some maladies of the skin'. Here is Gerard, three hundred years earlier: 'The women of our northern parts, especially about Wales and Cheshire, do tun the herbe Ale hoove into their ale.'

Ground Ivy Tea

(1) Gather the leaves in summer. Boil six or seven dried leaves in a pint of water. Strain and sweeten to taste.

(2) Use $\frac{1}{4}$ cup of freshly picked chopped leaves with 1 cup of water. Boil, strain and sweeten with syrup or honey.

❧ Hawthorn ❧

Crataegus monogyna (Rosaceae)

This is a native tree, common throughout Britain in woods and hedges. The white or pink blossoms come out in May and so the hawthorn is also known as the May-tree. Country people held that the flowers bore the sickly-sweet smell of the plague. In fact the smell is from the trimethylamine contained in them, which is an ingredient in the smell of putrefaction, and is what probably attracts the carrion insects mainly responsible for fertilising the hawthorn flowers.

In Roman times, hawthorn meant happiness and prosperity in marriage and it was believed to protect new-born children from sickness and evil. Later, in Christian times, it was reputedly used for Christ's crown of thorns and regarded as sacred. Superstitions remain: some people believe it unlucky to bring the blossoms indoors; some think it powerful against lightning; and there are strange beliefs attached to solitary thorns – legend tells us that the famous Glastonbury thorn sprouted from the staff of Joseph of Arimathea and burst into leaf every Christmas Eve. The tree is often associated with boundary marks, thorn hedges having been used to divide plots of land from early times. In Ireland there are sacred thorns by holy wells, frequently hung with favours –

usually odd scraps of material tied to the branches.

The leaves were once used to adulterate tea and an infusion of the flowers, taken two or three times a day, is considered good for palpitations, angina pectoris and circulation disorders.

HAWTHORN HERBAL TEA

Using 2 parts dried hawthorn leaves, 1 part lemon balm and 1 part sage, make tea as usual and infuse for several minutes. Sweeten with honey to taste.

HAWTHORN-BLOSSOM WINE

    2 quarts hawthorn blossom
    $2\frac{1}{2}$ lb sugar
    2 lemons
    1 gal water
    wine yeast and nutrient

Grate the rind from the lemons, avoiding all white pith, and boil in the water with the sugar and juice of one lemon for thirty minutes. Pour into a crock and, when lukewarm, add the yeast and nutrient. Leave for twenty-four hours, then add the flowers. Leave covered in a warm place for a week, stirring daily, then strain through muslin or a jelly bag into a fermentation jar. Fit an airlock, rack when clear and, after a second racking, bottle as usual.

HAWTHORN LIQUEUR
(Victorian recipe)

The full blossoms of the whitethorn are to be picked dry and clean from the leaves and stalks, and as much put into a large bottle as it will hold lightly without being pressed down. It is then to be filled up with French brandy and allowed to stand two or three months, when it must be decanted off, and sweetened with clarified sugar, or with capillaire. Without the sweetening it is an excellent seasoning for puddings and custards. [Capillaire was a syrup made from the maidenhair fern (*Asplenium adiantum nigrum*) but sometimes a simple syrup flavoured with orange-flower water was used instead.]

HAWTHORNBERRY LIQUEUR

Half-fill a Kilner jar with clean haws, add sugar to taste and fill up with brandy. Shake daily until the sugar is dissolved, leave for two or three months, strain and bottle.

❧ Heather ❧

Erica cinerea; Erica tetralix; Calluna vulgaris (Ericaceae)

The king in the red moorland
Rode on a summer's day;
And the bees hummed, and the curlews
Cried beside the way.
The king rode, and was angry,
Black was his brow and pale,
To rule in a land of heather
And lack the heather ale.

(R. L. Stevenson: *Heather Ale*)

Needless to say, heather is a popular emblem among the Scottish clans and the Menzies clan even have a variety named after them which grows only on a moorland in their own territory of Perthshire. With a rather different sense of scale, Gerard writes that 'heath groweth upon dry mountaines which are hungry and barren, as upon Hampstead Heath neere London'.

Bell heather, cross-leaved heath and ling are the commonest, the last being prized by bee-keepers for the thick dark honey it produces late in the year, and for which the hives are transported many miles. Ling is an evergreen and almost indestructible shrub: it has been used extensively for bedding, for thatching, for brooms and baskets, for fuel and to produce an orange dye. The flowering tips boiled in water are said to have antiseptic and diuretic qualities and, when added to the bath, to tone up the muscles and help rheumatic sufferers.

The tips were also used for centuries to make heather ale, about which there are many romantic stories. One of these is of a massacre of the Picts in the fourth century, the last survivor preferring to plunge to his death over a cliff rather than trade the secret of heather

ale for his life. But there are records of ale made from the tips of young heath mixed with a third part of malt and a few hops (Pennant 1774), and in the nineteenth century mention is made of heather being used in place of hops for beer-making in the Western Isles. We have been making heather ale for several years now, using sometimes the purple bell heather, sometimes the ling, and sometimes a mixture. It makes an excellent ale, strong and with a pronounced honey fragrance.

MOORLAND TEA
(associated with Robert Burns)

Mix together carefully dried heather tops, bramble leaves, and leaves of bilberry, speedwell, wild thyme and wild strawberry. Prepare as for China tea and sweeten, if you wish, with heather honey.

HEATHER ALE

1 gal heather tops
2 lb malt extract
1½ lb sugar
3 gals water
1 oz dried yeast

Cut the heather tops with scissors when in full bloom, but not overblown, and boil them in 1 gallon of the water for nearly an hour. Strain on to the malt extract and sugar through a jelly bag and stir till dissolved. Add remaining water and, when lukewarm, add the dried yeast. Cover with a cloth and leave in a warm

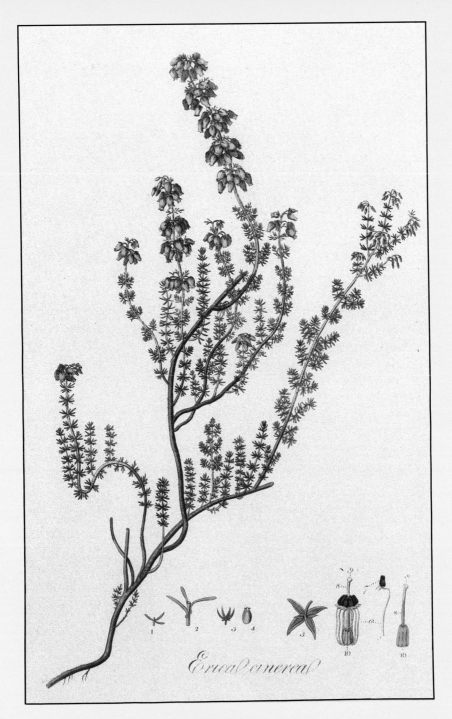

Erica cinerea

HEATHER

place for five or six days. Siphon into screw-top bottles, adding 1 teaspoon of sugar to each. Leave until clear before drinking and always decant carefully into a jug to avoid the sediment. Heather ale takes longer to clear than other ales, so be patient.

❧ Honeysuckle ☙

Lonicera periclymenum (Caprifoliaceae)

Although frequently cultivated in gardens, honeysuckle (or woodbine) is a native plant which grows anywhere in the British Isles where it can find support – and this includes half-way up cliff faces in the Cuillin of Skye, not the sort of environment imagined by Shakespeare:

> TITANIA: *Sleep thou, and I will wind*
> *thee in my arms . . .*
> *So doth the woodbine, the sweet honeysuckle*
> *Gently entwist . . .*
>
> *(Shakespeare:*
> *A Midsummer Night's Dream, IV, 1)*

The leaves were the only part used in Culpeper's day – 'put into gargarisms for sore throats' – but it is now known that the whole plant contains salicylic acid, the essential element in aspirin and other medicines. In France the flowers as well as the leaves are used and an infusion of these is recommended for children's coughs, especially whooping cough. But the berries, tempting though they look, can cause sickness and diarrhoea if taken in any quantity. Like mistletoe, the plant is magical:

> *O man that for Fergus of the feasts dost*
> *kindle fire,*
> *Whether afloat or ashore burn not the king*
> *of the woods.*

> *Monarch of Innisfail's forests the woodbine*
> *is, whom none may hold captive;*
> *No feeble sovereign's effort is it to hug all*
> *tough trees in his embrace.*
> *The pliant woodbine if thou burn, wailings*
> *for misfortune will abound*
> *Dire extremity at weapons' points or*
> *drowning in great waves will follow.*
> (Old Irish: translated by S. O'Grady)

HONEYSUCKLE TEA

Pick the flowers when in full bloom and dry them in the shade. Use $\frac{1}{2}$ oz to 1 pint of boiling water and infuse for ten minutes. Strain and sweeten with honey.

HONEYSUCKLE WINE

2 pints blossom (fully opened)
$2\frac{1}{2}$ lb sugar
1 orange
1 lemon
1 gal water
1 Camden tablet
wine yeast and nutrient

Place the flowers and Camden tablet in a crock and cover with $\frac{1}{2}$ gallon of boiling water. Add cold water to make up to 1 gallon. When

[52]

Lonicera Periclymenum.

HONEYSUCKLE

lukewarm, add the fruit juice and the thinly pared rind (avoiding the pith), the yeast and nutrient. Strain into a fermentation jar, fit an airlock and leave in a warm place to ferment. Rack when clear, then rack a second time and bottle as usual when fermentation has ceased.

❧ Hops ☙

Humulus lupulus (Cannabinaceae)

'Kent, sir — everybody knows Kent — apples, cherries, hops, and women.'
(Dickens: *Pickwick Papers*)

Hops are found wild in hedges in south and east England, more locally in Ireland and rarely in Scotland. The name *Humulus* comes from humus as hops usually indicate the presence of good soil. They are extensively cultivated for brewing, but only the flowers or cone-like catkins of the female hop plant are used for this.

The young shoots were used by the Romans as a vegetable and the flowers seem to have been used in breweries in the Netherlands at the beginning of the fourteenth century, although not until two hundred years later in England. Such plants as germander speedwell, woodsage, heather, ground ivy and yarrow had been used previously and, after the introduction of hops, *ale* remained the name for the old beverage and *beer* became the name for the new one, which at first met with great prejudice. But Gerard put in a sober word for hops: 'The manifold vertues of Hops do manifestly argue the holsomnesse of Beere above Ale; for the Hops rather make it a Phisicall drinke to keep the body in health, than an ordinarie drinke for the quenching of our thirst.'

Hops are tonic and diuretic, improve the appetite and promote sleep, and a pillow filled with them is said to be good for nervous irritation. Gerard wrote: 'The floures make bread light and the lump to be sooner and easilier leavened, if the meale be tempered with liquor wherein they have been boyled,' and beer added to the liquid in bread-making certainly has this effect.

HOP TEA

Infuse $\frac{1}{4}$ oz of dried hops in 1 pint of boiling water and leave for ten minutes before drinking.

BEER

2 oz dried hops
2 lb malt extract
$1\frac{1}{2}$ lb sugar
3 gals water
1 oz yeast

Boil the hops in half the water for thirty minutes, then strain on to the sugar and malt extract and stir till dissolved. Add the remaining water and, when lukewarm, add the dried yeast. Cover and leave to ferment for five or six days, then siphon off into clean screw-top bottles, adding 1 teaspoon of sugar to each bottle. Leave for at least a week before drinking.

[54]

Ale Posset
(Meg Dods; see also under Bog Myrtle)

Boil 1 pint of new milk with a slice of bread, sweeten and season a bottle of mild ale in a china basin or dish, and pour the boiling milk over it. When the head rises, serve it.

Het Pint
(Meg Dods)

Grate a nutmeg into 2 quarts of mild ale, and bring it to the point of boiling. Mix a little cold ale with a considerable quantity of sugar and 2 eggs well beaten. Gradually mix the hot ale with the eggs, taking care that they do not curdle. Put in ½ pint of spirits, and bring it once more nearly to the boil; and then briskly pour it from one vessel into another till it becomes smooth and bright. [Het pint was traditionally served at New Year.]

Ale Bitters

Steep in 1 gallon of ale 4 ounces each of gentian root and fresh lemon peel. After ten days, strain the liquor off and bottle it for use. (See also under Chamomile.)

King's Cup
1 quart strong Scotch ale
½ pint brandy
1 pint water
4 oz brown sugar
1 lemon
cloves, cinnamon, ginger, nutmeg to taste
2 slices toast

Dissolve the sugar in the water; slice the lemon into it and let it stand for fifteen minutes. Add the cloves and cinnamon, pour in the brandy and ale and stir well. Put in the toast, stir and sprinkle the nutmeg and ginger over it. This may be drunk warmed or iced and is taken chiefly at dinner.

❧ Juniper ☙
Juniperus communis (Cupressaceae)

A native evergreen shrub, juniper is common in Scotland, the Lake District, and south-east England in birch and pine woods and on moors and heaths. The berries, which you can buy quite easily, are well known as a flavouring for gin but they can also be used extensively in cooking — in marinades, courts-bouillon, pâtés and in sauerkraut and other vegetable dishes.

Medicinally, juniper is recommended for complaints of the urinary tract, being antiseptic and diuretic, and is also prescribed for arthritis and chronic rheumatism. It has been said that the inhabitants of northern countries protect themselves from these complaints by the frequent imbibing of spirits containing juniper berries — a course of treatment which crowns protection with oblivion. In such cases (i.e. of intoxication) you can fumigate the room and disinfect its inmates by boiling juniper berries in a pan, as with eucalyptus. Gerard, sober as usual, mentions that 'divers in Bohemia do take instead of other drinks, the water wherein

[55]

those berries have been steeped, who live in wonderful health'.

The wood was used in marquetry and veneering, for making cups and cabinets, and the bark was manufactured into ropes. The charcoal from this wood gives out the most durable heat and live embers have been found in the ashes after having been covered for twelve months.

When picking the berries (October to November) you will notice both green and blue berries on the bush, since they take two or three years to mature. Only the blue ones should be picked and they should then be spread out to dry, turned frequently and then stored in jars.

JUNIPER TEA

Pour 1 pint of boiling water on 1 oz of the crushed berries and leave to infuse for ten minutes. Drink three cups a day, sweetened with honey – and don't be upset if your urine turns violet!

JUNIPER WINE
(French recipe)

Macerate 1 oz of crushed berries in a bottle of good white wine for a fortnight, shaking occasionally; strain, sweeten with honey if desired, and take a wineglassful first thing in the morning for your general well-being.

JUNIPER RATAFIA
(Victorian recipe)

Take of juniper berries 3 oz, anise, coriander, cinnamon and cloves, of each 18 grains. Bruise all these ingredients and infuse them for a month in 3 pints of brandy; then strain it, add ¾ lb of sugar dissolved in ½ pint of water, stir them together, pass the whole through a jelly-bag, and bottle it. Keep well corked.

❧ Lime ❧

Tilia europea (Tiliaceae)

'It grows in parks and gentlemen's gardens,' writes Culpeper, and this is still true of our common lime which is a spontaneous hybrid, the native species from which it is derived being much less common. The flowers make a delicious tea popular on the continent, especially in France where it is known as *tilleul*; and the honey is considered the best-flavoured of all – and valuable in medicine and the manufacture of liqueurs. The wood is used quite extensively, being light, never attacked by worm, and suitable for fine carving. The Gibbons flower and figure carvings in St Paul's and Windsor Castle are of lime wood.

Lime flowers are used in infusion or made into a distilled water as a remedy for hysteria, migraines, palpitations and other nervous disorders; and the water in which the flowers have been boiled for fifteen minutes can be used as a face lotion to clear the skin.

'In the mean time, is there a more ravishing or delightful object, than to behold some entire streets and whole towns planted with these trees, in even lines before their doors, so as they seem like cities in a wood?' (John Evelyn: *Silva*.)

LIME-FLOWER TEA

Gather the flowers when in full bloom and dry them carefully. Make tea as you would China tea and sweeten with honey to taste; or use the fresh flowers. This is a known sedative, and prescribed for nervous indigestion and insomnia.

LIME-FLOWER WINE

1 quart lime flowers
$2\frac{1}{2}$ lb sugar
1 gal water
1 lemon
yeast and nutrient

Add the flowers and the thinly-pared lemon rind (without any pith) to the water and simmer for ten minutes. Strain the liquid on to the sugar and lemon juice and stir till dissolved. When lukewarm, add the yeast and nutrient, put into a fermentation jar, fit an airlock and leave in a warm place. Rack if necessary during the fermentation period, then, when fermentation has ceased and wine is clear, siphon off and bottle as usual.

❧ Marjoram ❧

Origanum vulgare (Labiatae)

Wild marjoram is found throughout the British Isles on calcareous soils on dry slopes, by roadsides and at the edges of woodlands, but is most common in the southern counties. It is a pretty aromatic plant with pale pinkish-purple flowers, and it is easily grown in the garden. Marjoram tea used to be common in Kent and 'swete' bags, 'swete' powders and 'swete' washing water were made from the plant. It was also added to ale before the introduction of hops, to add flavour and to help preserve it.

Gerard gives us many uses for the plant in case of poisoning, dropsy and coughs. Used in baths, he says, 'it healeth scabs, itches and scurvy,' and 'the weight of a dram taken with

Origanum vulgare.

MARJORAM

meade or honeyed water, draweth forth by stoole black and filthy humours, as Dioscorides and Pliny write'. Nowadays we know it as the herb used extensively in Italian cooking – on pizzas and in sauces and stuffings. It dries most successfully.

MARJORAM TEA

Carefully dry the leaves or the flowering tops and use 1 teaspoon per cup (or a little more if used fresh). Make as you would China tea, infuse for a few minutes, strain and sweeten with honey to taste. Good for headaches and nausea.

MARJORAM WINE

Macerate 1 oz of fresh marjoram in a bottle of good wine. Leave for a week and strain through a fine cloth. Drink a small glassful after meals.

❧ Meadowsweet ❧

Filipendula ulmaria (Rosaceae)

One of our most beautiful and delicate summer flowers, queen-of-the-meadows or meadow-sweet does indeed grow in damp meadows (and by streams and in ditches too), but it is from its former use as a flavouring for mead that it gets its name. In Gaelic it was known as the belt of Cuchullain, the Celtic hero whose legendary appalling spasms of rage may simply have been spasmodic fevers, for which meadow-sweet was a cure. The flowers were often put into wines or beers and are still an ingredient of country herb beers.

The perfume is sweet and heady, reminiscent of almond, and Gerard writes of one of the old common uses for it: 'The leaves and floures farre excell all other strowing herbs, for to decke up houses, to straw in chambers, halls, and banqueting houses in the summer time; for the smell thereof makes the heart merrie, delighteth the senses: neither doth it cause head-ache, or lothsomnesse to meat, as some other sweete smelling herbs do.'

The leaves as well as the flowers can be used for flavouring many sorts of drink and they used to be added to port and claret as well as mead. You can use the tea as a natural alternative to aspirin, for it contains the same active principle – salicylic acid.

MEADOWSWEET TEA

Strip the flowers from the stems, using a fork, and dry carefully. Prepare as you would China tea and sweeten with honey to taste.

MEADOWSWEET WINE

> 1 gal flowers
> $\frac{1}{2}$ lb raisins
> 1 lemon
> $\frac{1}{4}$ pint cold tea
> $2\frac{1}{2}$ lb sugar
> 1 gal water
> yeast and nutrient

Put the flowers in a stone crock and pour the

Spiræa Ulmaria

Meadowsweet

boiling water over them. Stir well, and leave for three days, stirring frequently. Strain the liquid on to the sugar and stir until dissolved. Add the chopped raisins, lemon juice, cold tea, yeast and nutrient. Put in a fermentation jar and leave in a warm place to ferment. Rack, and bottle when fermentation has ceased and wine is clear.

❦ Mint ❧

Mentha piperata; Mentha spicata; Mentha aquatica (Labiatae)

Tho wente I forth on my right hond
Doun by a lytel path I fond
Of mentes full, and fenell grene;
And faste by, without wene,
Sir Myrthe I fond, and right anoon
Unto Sir Myrthe gan I goon,
There as he was, hym to solace.
(Chaucer: *The Romaunt Of The Rose*)

The mint family is large and some are native plants, others introduced. The well-known spearmint (*M. spicata*) was probably brought here by the Romans; peppermint is a hybrid between *M. spicata* and *M. aquatica*; and M. *aquatica* (water mint) is abundant in wet places throughout Britain.

Peppermint is a common escape but also grows wild locally in moist places and by streams. Commercially, it is cultivated for the distillation of peppermint oil which is used for flavouring and in medicine. Peppermint tea, made with the dried herb, is a useful remedy and is good for influenza. Country people used it for colic or to induce sleep and it is also very refreshing and helps to allay nausea. This is the *menthe d'Angleterre* of the French and *Pfefferminze* or *englische Minze* of the Germans.

Of spearmint, Gerard says, 'The smell rejoiceth the heart of man, for which cause they use to strew it in chambers and places of recreation, pleasure and repose, where feasts and banquets are made;' but there are much earlier references too, from Roman and Old Testament times: 'Dioscorides teacheth, that being applied to the secret part of a woman before the act, it hindreth conception.' I am not a pupil of Dioscorides! Parkinson, in his *Garden of Pleasure*, says: 'Mintes are sometimes used in Baths with Balm and other herbs as a help to comfort and strengthen the nerves and sinews.'

All the mints are easily grown, but they prefer a moist situation. They have rampant root systems so it is a good idea to confine each variety in a bucket or similar receptacle buried in the ground.

PEPPERMINT TEA

Use the leaves and stems and pour boiling water over them. Infuse for a few minutes, then strain and sweeten with honey. Make spearmint tea in the same way, or dry carefully for winter mint tea.

[61]

Mentha hirsuta

MINT

MINT JULEP

Strip the tender leaves of mint into a tumbler and add to them as much wine, brandy, or any other spirit, as you wish to take. Put some pounded ice into a second tumbler, pour this on to the mint and brandy, and continue to pour the mixture from one tumbler to the other until the whole is sufficiently impregnated with the flavour of the mint, which is extracted by the particles of the ice coming into brisk contact when changed from vessel to vessel.

MINT PUNCH

Pick 1 quart of fresh mint leaves, and wash and dry them in a clean towel. Put them in a large jug and mash them with a wooden spoon till soft. Cover them with boiling water and infuse for ten minutes. Strain, cool and chill. Add 2 cups of chilled grape juice and lemon juice to taste. Sweeten with castor sugar, stir till dissolved and add 1 quart of ginger ale. Put some ice in each tumbler and fill up with the punch.

❧ Nettle ❧

Urtica dioica (Urticaceae)

I like the dust on the nettles, never lost
Except to prove the sweetness of a shower.
(Edward Thomas: *Tall Nettles*)

Keble Martin describes the nettle as 'too common'; it is certainly difficult to eradicate and neither beautiful nor fragrant. But the nettle chiefly flourishes where man has lived – so much so that, in a manner of speaking, we have domesticated it, and in any case we should welcome it as one of the most useful of plants. The young leaves, cooked like spinach or made into soups or soufflés, are a most delicious vegetable, and medicinally the nettle is still valued by country people as a spring tonic, for clearing the skin and as a remedy for children's bed-wetting. In Scotland, as in Germany and Scandinavia (see Hans Andersen's *The Princess and the Eleven Swans*), nettles were cut, dried and steeped, and the fibres separated, spun into yarn and woven into cloth. The poet Campbell (1777–1844), in *Letters from the South*, wrote: 'Be not nettled, my friend, at my praise of this useful weed. In Scotland I have eaten nettles, I have slept in nettle sheets and I have dined off a nettle table-cloth.'

Paper used to be made from nettles in France; a yellow dye can be got from boiling the roots with alum, and a green one from the leaves which are also used for a rinse to darken the hair. As fodder, the green part is valuable in the dried state, when it has lost its sting; hens lay better when it is powdered and added to their food; and animals are generally healthier with a proportion of nettles in their diet.

Vegetarian cheese-makers may be interested to know that a vegetable substitute for rennet can be obtained by boiling the leaves in a

[63]

strong solution of salt. A spoonful of this will curdle milk and leave no disagreeable taste, though of course the whey will be useless.

Use gloves when picking nettles and thoroughly wash them in several waters. The juice of the nettle itself soothes the irritation of the sting and every child knows that dock leaves are an antidote to the poison, especially when accompanied by the following incantation:

Nettle in, dock out,
Dock in, nettle out,
Nettle in, dock out,
Dock rub nettle out.

Nettle Tea

Boil young leaves in water for ten minutes, strain and sweeten with honey to taste; or use the leaves dried.

Nettle Wine

2 quarts young nettle tops
3 lb sugar
2 lemons
½ oz root ginger
1 gal water
wine yeast and nutrient

Wash the nettles thoroughly and simmer them in some of the water with thinly pared lemon peel and bruised ginger for forty-five minutes. Strain and make up the liquor to 1 gallon, using hot water. Pour this hot liquor on to the sugar in a stone crock and add lemon juice and nutrient. Stir till dissolved and, when the liquor is lukewarm, add the yeast. Cover the crock and leave in a warm place for four days, stirring daily. Transfer to a fermentation vessel and fit an airlock. When the wine begins to clear, rack into a clean jar and leave for three months before final bottling.

Nettle Beer

3 lb sugar
2 gal cold water
1 pailful of young nettle tops
3 or 4 handsful of young dandelion
3 or 4 handsful of goosegrass
2 oz bruised whole ginger
1 oz dried yeast

Boil the plants for ten minutes then strain on to the sugar in a stone crock. Stir until dissolved and, when lukewarm, add the yeast. Cover and leave in a warm place for five or six days, then siphon off into clean screw-top bottles adding 1 teaspoon sugar to each. Leave until clear.

Other herbs used to be added to nettle beer — meadowsweet, burdock or currant leaves — but sometimes the beer was made with nettles only.

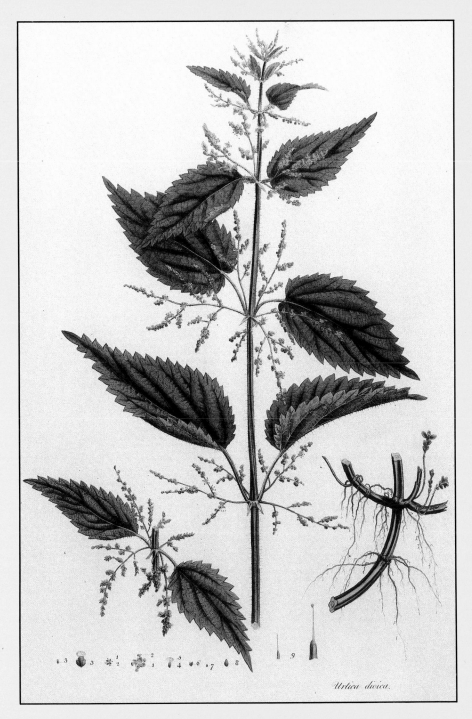

Urtica dioica.

NETTLE

❧ Oak ❧

Quercus robur (Fagaceae)

The oak has been closely associated with our history but, though thought of as primarily English, it used to be widespread in Scotland before its destruction for charcoal, and features on the badges of at least six clans. The name *Quercus* is said to be Celtic in origin, meaning 'fine tree', and the oak has been venerated since Druidic times and was adopted by the Christian religion:

> *Dearest, bury me*
> *Under that holy oke, or Gospel tree;*
> *Where, though thou see'st not, thou may'st*
> *think upon*
> *Me, when you yearly go'st Procession.*
> (Herrick: *To Anthea*)

But the oak has more down-to-earth uses and the acorns were used to feed pigs. 'They give them also to oxen, mingled with bran, chopped or broken, otherwise they are apt to sprout and grow in their bellies' (John Evelyn: *Sylva*). In Germany acorn coffee was the national beverage during the rationing of the First World War, and it is said to possess antiseptic properties. Last century Dr Barras found 'the infusion of roasted acorns, sweetened with sugar, of great advantage in promoting digestion if taken in the same way as coffee after meals' and he had seen 'dyspepsia and even disordered stomache cured by the use of them'. If his remedy should fail, you can always make a coffin out of the timber.

Oak-Leaf Tea
(French recipe)

Pick young leaves in the spring, dry carefully and use 1 oz to 1 pint of water. Boil for a few minutes, leave to infuse for ten minutes and drink sweetened with honey.

Acorn Coffee

Roast the acorns in a moderate oven till dark brown and thoroughly dry. Grind in a coffee grinder and prepare as you would coffee.

Oak-Leaf Wine

1 gal oak leaves
2½ lb sugar
juice of 2 lemons
1 gal water
wine yeast and nutrient

Bring 4 or 5 pints of the water to the boil and dissolve the sugar in it. Pour this over the leaves, infuse overnight and then strain into a fermenting vessel. Add lemon juice, nutrient and yeast, shake well, then top up with cold water to the bottom of the neck. Fit an airlock and leave in a warm place to ferment. When it clears, rack into another clean jar, and do this again before bottling.

❧ Primrose ❧

Primula vulgaris (Primulaceae)

PERDITA: . . . *pale primroses,*
That die unmarried, ere they can behold
Bright Phoebus in his strength, a malady
Most incident to maids; . . .
(Shakespeare: *A Winter's Tale*, IV, 3)

The name comes from the Latin *prima rosa*, first rose of the year. The primrose is still plentiful in many places, though near the cities it is sadly overpicked. It flowers on banks, railway embankments and in moist places, often right down to the edge of the sea. The whole herb was used in country medicine, having similar properties to those of the cowslip, and it was considered 'an important remedy in muscular rheumatism, paralysis and gout' (Grieve: *A Modern Herbal*). It seems a shame to pick primroses in the vast quantities needed for wine unless you grow them in your garden: but primrose tea is pleasant and is said to 'cure the phrensie'.

'Of the leaves of Primrose is made as fine a salve to heal a wound as any I know' (Culpeper); and you can also make jam with the flowers, or candy them as you can violet or borage flowers.

'I could have brought you some primroses, but I do not like to mix violet with anything.'

'They say primroses make a capital salad,' said Lord St Jerome.

(Disraeli: *Lothair*)

Primrose Tea

To each cup of petals use 7 cups of water and infuse in the usual way. Strain and sweeten with honey to taste.

Primrose Wine

1 gal primrose flowers
3 lb sugar
2 oranges
1 lemon
1 gal water
wine yeast and nutrient

Boil the water, stir in the sugar and add the thinly pared rinds of the oranges and lemon (avoiding the pith), the flowers and the fruit juice. When lukewarm add the nutrient and

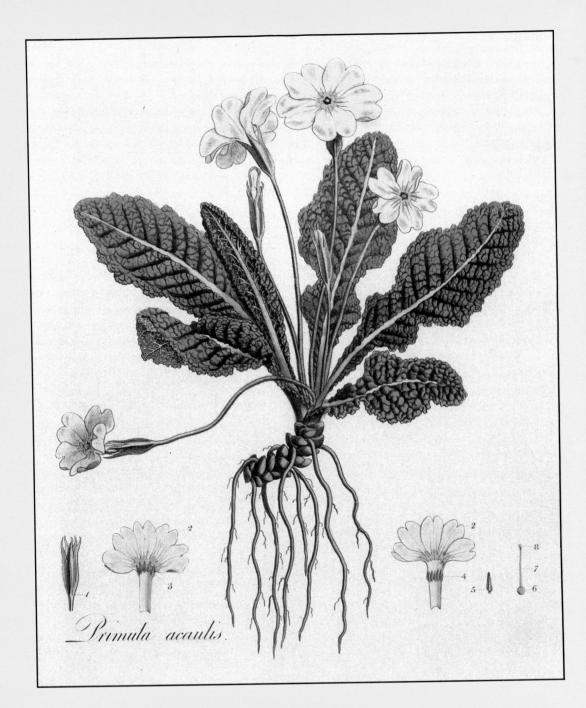

Primula acaulis.

PRIMROSE

yeast and leave covered in a warm place for five days, stirring daily. Strain into a fermentation jar, fit an airlock and leave to ferment. Rack after about three months, and then again after another three months or so, before finally bottling.

✀ Raspberry ✀

Rubus idaeus (Rosaceae)

The 'bramble of Mount Ida' is still called the hindberry in some parts of England and Scotland as it is a favourite of the deer. Smaller than the cultivated raspberry, it has a fresher and sharper flavour and associations with childhood which would probably make it taste better anyway:

> *Where mid the gorse the raspberry*
> *Red for the gatherer springs,*
> *Two children did we stray and talk*
> *Wise, idle, childish things.*
> (Francis Thompson : *Daisy*)

Culpeper tells us that 'the juice of the ripe fruit boiled into a syrup, with refined sugar, is pleasant and agreeable to the stomache and prevents sickness and retchings'. Country people have long used an infusion of the dried leaves as a gargle for sore throats or, for its astringent properties, in children's stomach upsets.

RASPBERRY-LEAF TEA

This is a remedy for chills and influenza. Use 1 oz of dried leaves to 1 pint of water. Make it as you would China tea and take sweetened with honey.

RATAFIA OF RASPBERRIES
(Victorian recipe)

Take 3 pints of raspberry juice and $\frac{1}{2}$ pint of cherry juice: dissolve in these $1\frac{1}{2}$ lb of fine sugar, and let it stand some time; then add 3 quarts of the best brandy, strain it, and when quite clear, bottle it. Be careful to keep it well corked.

RASPBERRY BRANDY
(old recipe)

Pick fine dry fruit, put it into a stone jar, and the jar into a kettle of water, or on a hot hearth, till the juice will run; strain, and to every pint add $\frac{1}{4}$ lb of sugar, bring it to the boil and skim it; when cold, mix equal quantities of juice and brandy, shake well and bottle.

[69]

RASPBERRY WINE
(Victorian recipe)

Pound the fruit and strain it through a cloth; then boil as much water as you have of juice, and when cold pour it on the dry fruit, letting it stand five hours, after which strain it again, and mix it with the rest. To every gallon of this liquor add 2½ lb of sugar, let it stand in an earthenware vessel closely covered for a week, and then tun it into a clean cask; bung it well, and when fine bottle it off. [Use a proper wine yeast for good results.]

❧ Rose ☙

Rosa canina; Rosa arvensis; Rosa rubiginosa; Rosa spinosissima; Rosa villosa (Rosaceae)

These are all the indigenous roses of the British Isles, the burnet rose (*R. spinosissima*) and the downy rose (*R. villosa*) being more common in the north. The dog rose (*R. canina*) is particularly sought after for its hips, but the hips of all the varieties can be used, as can the petals. The burnet rose is the most strongly scented, the dog rose more delicate and the sweetbriar (*R. rubiginosa*) valued for its perfumed foliage. 'The fruit when it is ripe maketh most pleasant meats and banqueting dishes, as tarts and such-like; the making whereof I commit to the cunning cook' (Gerard). You can also make rose-petal jams, syrups, vinegars, salads and a tea with the dried leaves. The hips are extremely rich in vitamin C, having more than any other fruit or vegetable, and rose-hip syrup is well worth making for flavouring or as a pleasant hot drink in the winter. On the continent jam is sometimes made deliberately including the down of the hips to act as a cure for worms – and of course you can make pot-pourri and with ' . . . quick effluvia darting thro' the brain,/Die of a rose in aromatic pain . . .' (Pope: *Essay on Man*).

ROSE-HIP TEA

Top and tail the hips, make sure they are clean and dry, and spread out in a roasting tin. Place in a slow oven until absolutely dry, then grind in an electric coffee grinder and store in an airtight jar. Using about 1 teaspoon per cup, prepare as you would Indian tea, leaving to infuse for six or seven minutes, and strain through a very fine strainer.

ROSE-PETAL TEA

Pour 4 cups of boiling water over 3 teaspoons of dried rose petals. Infuse for three to five minutes and sweeten with honey to taste.

ROSE-HIP SYRUP

Quickly grate or chop 1 lb of rosehips and put immediately into 3 pints of boiling water. Simmer them for no more than five minutes and then leave to stand for fifteen minutes. Strain and measure and add about 10 oz of sugar to each pint of juice. When the sugar is

Rosa canina.

ROSE

dissolved, pour into pre-heated bottling jars (do not fill too full) and allow to cool. Stand the jars on a cloth or wooden rack in a large pan, slacken the screw-bands slightly from the tight position, then *very slowly* bring to simmering point and hold at that for twenty to thirty minutes, depending on the bottle size. Remove carefully on to a wooden surface and tighten the screw band. This method helps to retain the vitamin C.

ROSE-PETAL WINE

2 quarts scented rose petals
2½ lb sugar
1 lemon
1 gal water
wine yeast and nutrient

Bring the water to the boil and pour it over the rose petals, sugar and lemon juice. Stir well and, when lukewarm, add yeast and nutrient. Leave to ferment for a week in a warm place, keeping well covered and stirring daily. Then strain into a fermentation jar, fit an airlock and, when a firm deposit has formed, rack into a clean jar. When fermentation has ceased and wine is clear, siphon off into bottles. Leave for six months.

ROSE-HIP WINE

2 lb rose hips
1 tsp citric acid
2¾ lb sugar
1 gal water
pectic enzyme
wine yeast and nutrient

Wash the rose hips and either cut them in half or crush them. Put the sugar in a crock, add the hips and pour the boiling water over them. Stir well to dissolve the sugar. When lukewarm add the yeast, acid, enzyme and nutrient. Leave in a warm place, closely covered, for two weeks, stirring daily. Strain through a jelly-bag into a fermentation jar and fit an airlock. When the wine clears (after about three months) siphon off into a fresh jar and leave for another three months before bottling.

❧ Rowan ❧

Sorbus aucuparia (Rosaceae)

'*Tis but folly to scan the holly or more lofty*
trees,
When in the bushes where water rushes
we find heart's ease.
Though the rowan so high is growing, its
berry is tart,
While near the ground fruit sweet and
sound will charm the heart.
(Old Irish : translated by D. O'Sullivan)

The rowan, mountain ash or quicken is a native of the north and west where it grows at a higher altitude than any other British tree. It is found in woods and scrub, by mountain streams and even in sheltered gullies high up cliff faces, where it is often partnered by holly and, occasionally, by honeysuckle. Throughout the British Isles, Scandinavia and Iceland rowans were trees of protection and in Scotland you will find them planted round houses along with the equally powerful elder.

Some believed the rowan would keep the dead from rising; it was planted in graveyards, especially in Wales, and in the Highlands it was made into coffins. The tree was also used for a black dye and the wood cut into hoops for barrels. The berries make a delicious jelly for serving with game or wild fowl; and they are said to have anti-scorbutic qualities and were used in the past to treat scurvy. 'Ale and beer brewed with these berries, being ripe, is an incomparable drink, familiar in Wales, where the tree is reputed to be sacred,' writes Evelyn in *Sylva*, and 'the berries are such a tempting bait for the thrushes that as long as they last you can be sure of their company'.

ROWANBERRY LIQUEUR
(Victorian recipe)

1 pint brandy
1 pint clear syrup
1 handful rowanberries

The berries must be dried till shrivelled, then placed in brandy and left for seven to ten days. Then strain, and mix with an equal quantity of thick, very clear syrup made with loaf sugar in a brass boiler. Bottle.

ROWANBERRY WINE

3 lb rowanberries
1 lb raisins
$\frac{1}{2}$ lb wheat
$2\frac{3}{4}$ lb sugar
1 gal water
1 tablespoon citric acid
yeast and nutrient

Place the berries in a crock and pour the boiling water over them. Leave covered for four days, then strain. Add the sugar, acid, wheat and chopped raisins and stir till sugar is dissolved. Then add the yeast and nutrient. Leave closely covered for two weeks, then strain into a fermentation jar, fit an airlock, and leave in a warm place. When clear, siphon off into a clean jar and, when fermentation has ceased and wine is clear, bottle as usual.

❧ Speedwell ☙

Veronica chamaedrys (Scrophulariaceae)

The speedwells are a large family, but the commonest in the British Isles is germander speedwell which you can find on grassy banks and in clearings and meadows in spring and early summer.

There are numerous arguments as to how it got its name *Veronica*, which means 'true image'. In Wales it is sometimes called 'Christ's eye', and the idea of the true image is carried on in some English traditions in which your mother will be blinded if you pick it. In Germany it is known as *Blumchen der Treue* and picking it is believed to cause storms.

The leaves of speedwell are bitter and astringent and used often to be made into tea, especially on the continent – indeed the French call it *thé de l'Europe*.

Before Chinese tea acquired a settled reputation here, this, as well as several other plants, was recommended as a safe and pleasant beverage, and Swedish and German writers had also a high opinion of speedwell tea, which is said to be good for coughs. Perhaps then you are safe enough if you pick the leaves only!

Of its other 'vertues' Gerard writes: 'Germander boiled in water and drunk, delivereth the bodie from all obstructions or stoppings, divideth and cutteth tough and clammy humours . . . it provoketh mightily the termes, being boiled in wine and the decoction drunk; with a fomentation or broth made also thereof, and the secret parts bathed therewith.'

SPEEDWELL TEA

Dry the leaves carefully and prepare as you would China tea, infusing for several minutes and sweetening with honey to taste.

❧ Spruce Fir ☙

Picea abies (Pinaceae)

From John Evelyn's *Sylva* (1678): 'The Spruce Fir is a beautiful tree, as well as a valuable one for its timber, producing the white deal. It is a native of Norway and Denmark, where it grows spontaneously. . . . It also grows plentifully in the Highlands of Scotland, where it adorns those cloud-capped mountains with a constant verdure.'

This tree, known as the Norway spruce, is the conifer used as our Christmas tree and it is widely planted as it withstands frost and shade and has a fast growth rate. It was part of our native flora before it was exterminated in the pleistocene glaciations (one million years ago); it was re-introduced in the sixteenth century.

Spruce beer has been made from early times

Veronica Chamædrys.

SPEEDWELL

and was popular in the Highlands of Scotland:

Sweeter to me her kissing lip
Than the honey and the spruce-tree beer
Though we twain the mead were to sip
From two glasses together here!
(Gaelic: translated by G. McLean)

It is a purifier of the blood and a powerful anti-scorbutic – the essence used to be taken by sailors on long voyages so that they could brew beer as they required it.

SPRUCE BEER

2 lb malt essence or molasses
2 tablespoons essence of spruce
2 gals water (spring water if available)
1 oz dried yeast

Dissolve the malt or molasses in 1 gallon of warm water. Then add the essence of spruce, and when the mixture is tepid, sprinkle the dried yeast over it. Leave the cask closely covered for a few days until the fermentation subsides, then bung it firmly. It will be ready to syphon off into screw-top bottles in a week. You can buy spruce essence in most home-brew shops, but if you want to use the branches and cones, boil them for two hours, after which the liquor should be strained into a crock and the molasses or malt added.

SPRUCE ESSENCE

Gather the young shoots in the spring, put them in a large pan, cover with water and boil until the resinous flavour is extracted and the water is brown. Strain and return to the pan. Boil again until it is reduced by half, then bottle. (The outer sprigs and cones can also be used.)

❧ Strawberry ☙

Fragaria vesca (Rosaceae)

ELY: *The strawberry grows underneath*
the nettle:
And wholesome berries thrive and
ripen best,
Neighbour'd by fruit of baser quality . . .
(Shakespeare: *Henry V*, I, 1)

Personally I don't class the nettle as being of baser quality, but wild strawberries will grow under them, especially on calcareous soil and on grassy banks and the edges of woods and railway embankments, and will survive in quite dense cover.

Tea made from the dried leaves is astringent and used in cases of diarrhoea. Of the berries, Culpeper says: 'They cool the liver, the blood, and the spleen, or a hot choleric stomach; refresh and comfort failing spirits and quench thirst.'

STRAWBERRY-LEAF TEA

Dry perfect strawberry leaves and use as you would China tea. Infuse for a few minutes and sweeten with honey if desired.

❧ Tansy ☙

Chrysanthemum vulgare (Compositae)

Tansy is highly aromatic and refreshing and was used as a strewing herb in the Middle Ages for repelling mice and insects and to preserve dead bodies. It is common on hedge banks, by roadsides and in waste places. Medicinally, it was used to expel worms in children and generally to purge the system, especially after the limited salt-fish diet of Lent – a fast which happily coincided with a time of natural dearth. Sometimes tansy was collected by country people to make wine which was thought to have valuable remedial effects, and in Scotland a mild decoction of the plant was used as a medicine for gout.

The Revd Johns wrote in 1878: 'The whole plant is bitter and aromatic and is not only used in medicine but forms the principal ingredient in the nauseous dish called Tansy pudding.' But Culpeper says: 'Let those Women that desire Children love this Herb, 'tis their best Companion, their Husband excepted.' Personally I think that some of the old recipes for tansies would be worth reviving. They were generally eaten on Easter day, the custom having acquired a symbolic significance in memory of the bitter herbs eaten by the Jews at the Passover.

TANSY TEA

Use $\frac{1}{2}$ to 1 teaspoonful of the dried flowers and seeds infused for a few minutes and sweetened with honey. The leaves can also be used, but if you take them fresh you will only need about one frond-like leaf for a small pot.

Tansy Wine

1 large handful tansy leaves and flowers
1 lemon
$2\frac{3}{4}$ lb sugar
4 lb parsnips
$\frac{1}{4}$ pint cold tea
1 gal water
wine yeast and nutrient

Scrub and slice the parsnips and cook in the water till tender. Strain the liquid into a crock containing the sugar. Place the tansy in a pan, cover with water, bring to the boil and simmer for a few minutes, then strain on to the parsnip liquor and add the cold tea and lemon juice. When lukewarm add the nutrient and yeast, transfer to a fermentation jar and bottle when fermentation has ceased.

❧ Thyme ☙

Thymus serpyllum; Thymus drucei (Labiatae)

These are both native plants, *T. drucei* being more generally widespread, and the presence of wild thyme is believed to denote a pure atmosphere. The name *serpyllum* comes from a Greek word meaning 'to creep' – this on account of the plant's trailing habits. It is extremely hardy, much loved by bees – I have seen bumble bees working the wild thyme at well over 3,000 feet; indeed they were nesting under it on top of a mountain. It was supposed by the Highlanders to give courage and strength but was also associated with death and love. Young girls would wear sprigs of thyme, lavender and mint to bring them sweethearts; but in Wales they plant it on graves.

'A strong infusion, drank as tea, is pleasant and a very effectual remedy for head-ache, giddiness and other disorders of that kind; and a certain remedy for that troublesome complaint, the nightmare' (Culpeper).

Wild Thyme Tea

This is said to be useful in cases of drunkenness. Make tea as usual with the dried flowering tips, using one or two sprigs per cup. Sweeten with honey to taste. You can also mix the thyme with wild strawberry or raspberry leaves.

Thymus Serpyllum.

THYME

✄ Violet ✀

Viola odorata (Violaceae)

This sweet-scented violet appears very early in spring, usually with deep purple flowers, though they are occasionally pale rose-coloured or lilac. The flowers have been used since ancient times for medicinal and cosmetic purposes, or simply for posies, which were frequently associated with the death of the young.

> LAERTES: *. . . lay her i' the earth;*
> *And from her fair and unpolluted flesh*
> *May violets spring!*
>   (Shakespeare, *Hamlet*, V, 1)

The violet is found with other sweet-smelling herbs, such as thyme, in Welsh graveyards, and Romans set aside days (*dies violaris*) for decking their graves with flowers.

> *Lilies for a bridal bed,*
> *Roses for the matron's head,*
> *Violets for a maiden dead.*
>   (Shelley)

Preparations and dishes of violets were popular in Victorian England and there are also many French recipes. For a cure for insomnia here is a recipe from Askham's *Herbal*: 'For thē that may not slepe for sicknesse seeth this herbe in water and at even let him soke wel hys fete in the water to the ancles, whā he goeth to bed, bind of this herbe to his temples.'

SYRUP OF VIOLETS
(Victorian recipe)

Take of sweet violet flowers fully in bloom 4 ounces, and soak them in 16 ounces of boiling water for twenty-four hours in a covered glass or earthenware vessel. Strain the liquor from the flowers, and dissolve it in 30 ounces of fine loaf sugar.

VIOLET-FLOWER TEA

Use 2 teaspoonsful of dried violets to 1 pint of boiling water. Infuse for several minutes, strain and sweeten with honey if wished.

VIOLET SHRUB

Steep violet petals in a bottle of good white wine for a week. Strain, add fresh petals and leave for another week. Strain again and, before serving, add a little honey.

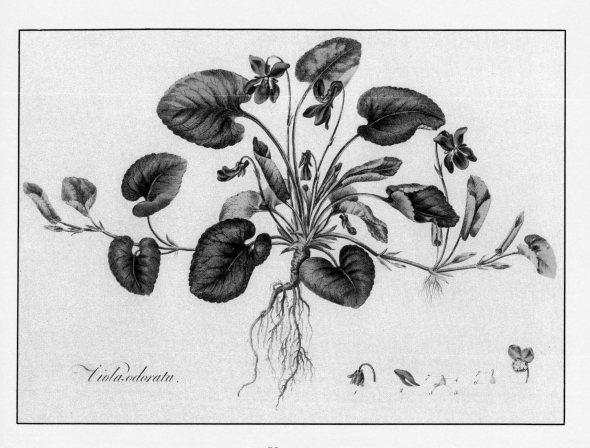

Viola odorata.

VIOLET

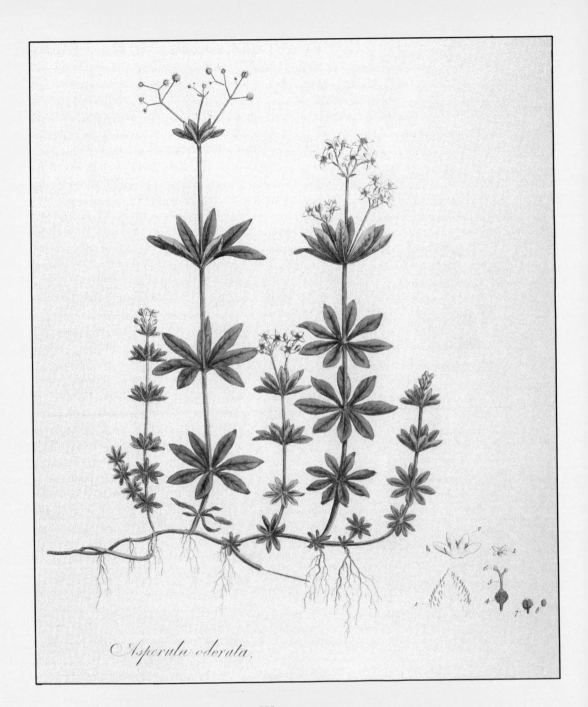

Asperula odorata.

WOODRUFF

❧ Woodruff ❧

Galium odoratum (Rubiaceae)

This pretty little plant, which is related to goosegrass (but does not cling), grows in moist shady places. The name appears as Wuderove in the thirteenth century, later Wood-rove, 'rove' being derived from the French *rovelle* (a wheel), in allusion to the spoke-like arrangement of the leaves. As it dries, it develops the delicious smell of hay and Gerard wrote of garlands of woodruff hung up in the houses in summer and which 'doth very wel attemper the aire, coole and make fresh the place, to the delight and comfort of such as are therein'. The dried herb was also kept among linen, strewn in churches in the Middle Ages, and used for stuffing beds.

In Germany a favourite hock cup is still made by steeping the fresh sprigs in Rhine wine and then mixing in an equal quantity of champagne – this is known as *Maibowle* and is traditionally drunk on 1 May. The fresh or dried herb is excellent steeped for a day or two in elderflower wine, or added to summer wine cups.

WOODRUFF TEA

Use the dried leaves and prepare as you would China tea. Sweeten with honey to taste. Said to be good for insomnia and nervous irritation.

❧ Woodsorrel ❧

Oxalis acetosella (Oxalidaceae)

'The woodsorrel with its light green leaves/ Heart-shaped, and triply folded; and its root/ Creeping like beaded coral' is a delicate but strongly flavoured plant, formerly known as sorrell du bois, which often carpets pine woods and other shady places. It was probably the plant used by St Patrick to demonstrate the concept of the Holy Trinity – though the Druids also revered it.

Woodsorrel was cultivated in the kitchen garden in the sixteenth century and the leaves were used to make a green sauce taken with fish. It was called Alleluia because, as Turner explained, it 'appeareth about Easter when

Alleluia is song again' and it is called *Alleluja* in Italy to this day. It can be used for sauces, soups and salads, and in Russia it was used to make a cooling drink said to help in cases of fever. Like the other sorrels it should not be taken in large quantities because of its high content of oxalic acid.

WOODSORREL AND BALM LEMONADE
(old recipe)

Put two sprigs of balm and a little woodsorrel into a stone jug, having first washed and dried

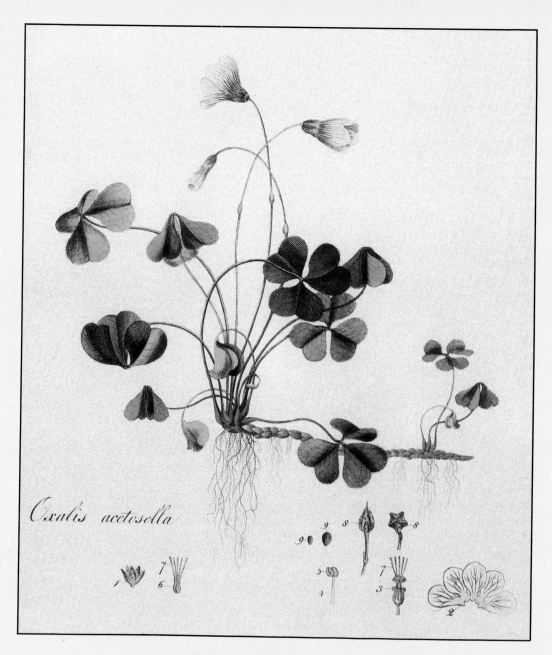

Oxalis acetosella

WOODSORREL

them; peel then a small lemon and clear from the white, slice it and put a bit of peel in; then pour in 3 pints of boiling water, sweeten and cover it close.

Woodsorrel Lemonade

Boil leaves for fifteen minutes, cool, strain and add honey or sugar and lemon juice to taste.

❧ Yarrow ☙

Achillea millefolium (Compositae)

'I will pick the smooth yarrow that my figure may be more elegant, that my lips may be warmer, that my voice may be more cheerful; may my voice be like a sunbeam, may my lips be like the juice of the strawberries. May I be an island in the sea, may I be a hill on the land, may I be a star when the moon wanes, may I be a staff to the weak one: I shall wound every man, no man shall wound me.' (Gaelic: translated by K. Jackson, *A Celtic Miscellany*, Penguin Books 1971).

Yarrow was regarded as a magical herb and used for healing wounds, getting its name from Achilles' use of it for his soldiers. It was used as a wound-salve in the Highlands and Ann Pratt mentions that the women of the Orkneys held 'milfoil' tea in high repute for its power of dispelling melancholy. The mountaineers of the Alps made vinegar of a dwarf species of yarrow and its flavour is held to be equal to that of tarragon. Gerard calls it nose-bleed and in parts of England it is still known by that name (in France is it called *saigne-nez*). 'The leaves being put into the nose, do cause it to bleed and ease the paine of the megrim.'

Culpeper, on the other hand, writes: 'As a medicine it is drying and binding. A decoction boiled with white wine is good to stop the running of the reins in men, and whites in women; restrains violent bleedings, and is excellent for the piles.' But aside from these no doubt useful functions, yarrow tea is bracing, good and warming in cold weather. In Sweden it is called field hop and has been used to make beer there – Linnaeus considered yarrow beer to be more intoxicating than that made with hops. The results of our experiments are inconclusive!

Yarrow Tea

This is a good remedy for colds. Place dry or green leaves in a cup, pour hot water over them, steep only until the colour shows and drink sweetened with honey.

Yarrow Beer

10 oz malt extract
8 oz sugar
4 oz dried yarrow leaves (a little more if using them fresh)
1 gal water
1 dessertspoon dried yeast

Boil the yarrow leaves in the water for thirty minutes. Strain on to the malt and sugar in a stone jar. Stir well till dissolved and, when lukewarm, sprinkle on the yeast. Cover with a cloth and leave in a warm place to ferment for five or six days. Siphon the beer off the sediment into screw-top bottles. Leave for at least a week before drinking.

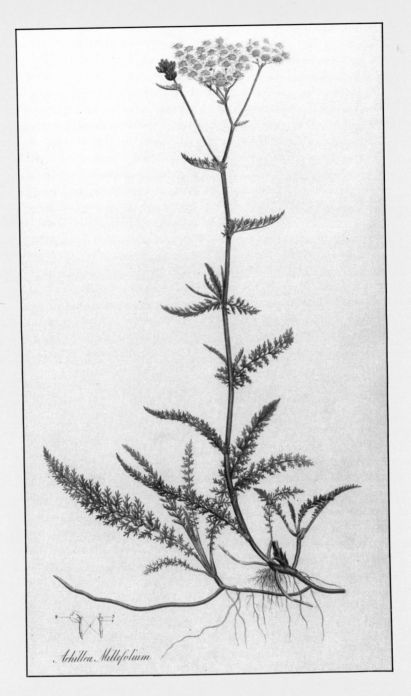

Achillea Millefolium

YARROW

❦ Selected Bibliography ❧

A. Askham: *Herbal* (1550)

The Book of the Household: numerous authors (undated: approx 1860)

Thomas Cogan: *The Haven of Health* (1596)

Nicholas Culpeper: *The English Physitian Enlarged* (1669)

William Curtis: *Flora Londinensis* (1777)

Meg Dods: *The Cook and Housewife's Manual* (1826)

John Evelyn: *Sylva, or a Discourse of Forest-Trees* (1644)

John Evelyn: *Acetaria, A Discourse of Sallets* (1699)

John Gerard: *The Herbal or General Historie of Plants* (1597)

John Gerard: *The Herbal, Enlarged and Amended, by Thomas Johnson* (1633)

Mrs Grieve: *A Modern Herbal* (1931)

Geoffrey Grigson: *The Englishman's Flora* (1958)

Revd W. Keble Martin: *A Concise British Flora* (1965)

F. Marian McNeill: *The Scots Cellar* (1956)

John Parkinson: *Theatrum Botanicum* (1640)

Roger Phillips: *Wild Flowers of Britain* (1977)

William Turner: *A New Herball* (1551)

Lady Wilkinson: *Weeds and Wild Flowers* (1858)

BALM

METRIC CONVERSION TABLE

$\frac{1}{4}$ oz	=	7.09 grams
$\frac{1}{2}$ oz	=	14.18 grams
1 oz	=	28.35 grams
8 oz	=	226.80 grams
1 lb	=	454.00 grams

$\frac{1}{2}$ pint	=	0.285 litres
1 pint	=	0.57 litres
1 quart	=	1.14 litres
1 gallon	=	4.54 litres

1 level teaspoon	=	5 mls
1 level tablespoon	=	15 mls

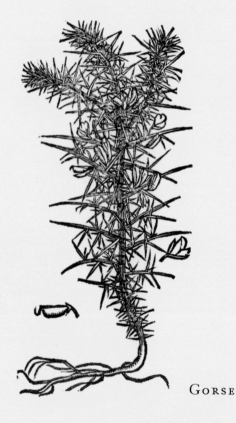

GORSE